The Secret to Navigating Life's Storms

The Secret to Navigating Life's Storms

Terry Lyles, PhD.

 Unless otherwise identified, Scripture quotations are from the King James Version of the Bible. Please note that Destiny Image's publishing style capitalizes certain pronouns in Scripture that refer to the Father, Son, and Holy Spirit, and may differ from some Bible publishers' styles.

Take note that the name satan and related names are not capitalized. We choose not to acknowledge him, even to the point of violating grammatical rules.

Destiny Image® Publishers, Inc.
P.O. Box 310
Shippensburg, PA 17257-0310

"Speaking to the Purposes of God for This Generation and for the Generations to Come"

ISBN 0-7684-2188-8

For Worldwide Distribution
Printed in the U.S.A.

2 3 4 5 6 7 8 9 10 11 12 13 14 15 / 09 08 07 06 05 04 03

ACKNOWLEDGMENTS

Special thanks to my family, Sandy, Brandon, and Brent for always living in my heart and inspiring me to be my best everyday. To Migdalia Cruz for her ability to control my schedule and to complete project details in a timely fashion. To my extended family, friends, and colleagues who always believed in the vision and inspiration of this book to touch the world with the needed message of life-balance. And, finally, I thank God every day for His love and grace extended toward me that has empowered me to accept the disability of my son, Brandon, without which I would not be where I am today. Also, a special thanks to Destiny Image for its dedication and passion to make the world a better place through literate means.

ENDORSEMENTS

The Secret to Navigating Life's Storms is an enlightening work on the realities of everyday life storms, which can cripple or empower depending on the response. Dr. Terry Lyles has found the formula to help all of us live above our fears, frustrations, and anxieties that life storms often bring.

Robert Polito
National Champion Penn State Football Player.

When we experience life's storms they can paralyze us. These storms interfere with our work, our relationships, and our overall feeling of well-being. Bravo for Dr. Lyles's excellent book that teaches us how to effectively navigate through these storms and get on with our lives—even through the most stressful and troubling of times. This book is a must for physicians, practitioners, and patients.

Shari Lieberman, Ph.D.
CNS, FACN, Nutrition Scientist, Exercise Physiologist

Dr. Terry Lyles's book is like no other personal growth or self-help title out there. He effectively uses his skills as a performance psychologist to convey successful strategies based in spirituality to achieve dramatic results for his readers.

Steve Friedman
President, PAX Cable

All business leaders are searching for the key to help themselves and their organizations sustain peak performance. Dr. Terry Lyles has found it in his understanding of how you align yourself mentally, emotionally, spiritually, and physically to master the stresses of life.

Rudy Borneo
Vice Chairman, Macy's West

Dr. Lyles has used the experiences of his life's journey to help us along our own paths. Stress can be debilitating and feared. Or, it can help us make a positive difference in our own lives and in those of others. He attacks his subject with a heart-felt passion to which all should heed.

Tim Pendell
Senior Director of Community Affairs
Detroit Lions, Inc.

Simply put, Dr. Terry Lyles's program changed my life in so many ways. As a Type One diabetic, the nutritional/physical part played a key role that resulted in better performance at work and at home. Balance is the key. Thanks Terry....

John Kamovitch
Senior Director, Management Development
Pfizer, Inc.

Dr. Terry Lyles has written the classic on navigating life's storms. I have been through many storms in my life and thought that I had learned the answers about dealing with them. After reading this book, I realized how much more I have learned. I know that you'll feel the same way after reading this powerful material.

Pat Williams
Senior Vice President, Orlando Magic

I heard Dr. Lyles speak and I was completely captivated. Here was a guy who understands the pressures and stress of life in the 21st century and how to deal with it, whether you are an athlete, executive, student, or mother. He nails our life management issues!

Scott Sharp
Indianapolis 500 Pole Winner

Life storms come and life storms go. Dr. Terry Lyles reinforces the need for balance in your life and equips the student with the tools to weather life's storms. Dr. Lyles' emphasis–taking care of self–plays a great part in balancing the mental, emotional, spiritual, and physical aspects in life.

Charlene M. Gasparovich
Manager, AME Training
DaimlerChrysler

Contents

Chapter One

Stressology: The Study of Life Storm Navigation

Courage is resistance to fear, mastery of fear, not absence of fear. Except a creature be part coward, it is not a compliment to say it is brave...

–Mark Twain

On the morning of September 11, 2001, I was in the airport in Fort Lauderdale, Florida, waiting to board my flight to Detroit, where I was to train management employees at a major automotive company. A commotion in a nearby restaurant drew my attention as customers scrambled for a closer view of the overhead television monitor. In stunned disbelief we watched as flames and dark smoke poured from the upper stories of the north tower of the World Trade Center in Manhattan. At this stage, no one knew that terrorists were responsible. The earliest reports were that a commuter aircraft had accidentally crashed into the building.

In a state of collective paralysis, we kept our eyes glued to the screen as more information came to light and it became clear that a commercial airliner was involved. Transfixed in shock and horror, we witnessed the unthinkable unfolding before our eyes as a second passenger jet, United Airlines Flight 175, slammed into the south tower. Immediately I thought, *This was no accident; this is war!* My mind was racing. I fly three to four days a week, and I wondered what I would have done if I had been on that plane.

The longer we watched, the worse it got. First, we heard about a third plane crashing into the Pentagon, and a fourth, into the Pennsylvania countryside. Then, in a scene so unimaginable as to seem almost surreal, we saw first the south tower and, 24 minutes later, the north tower of the World Trade Center collapse into immense piles of twisted, smoking rubble.

It was then that my training kicked in.

Immediately I realized that I had spent the last 20 years of my life preparing for this moment. Everything I had done during those years, from receiving quasi-military training in Alaska, to earning a Ph.D. in psychology, to field work with a leading sports science training center, had equipped me to respond to this crisis.

Within minutes of the attacks in New York and Washington, the airport in Fort Lauderdale closed, as did airports all across the country. No flights were coming in or going out. Since I knew I would not be flying to Detroit, I called home to West Palm Beach and told my wife, Sandy, that I was driving to our church instead.

Ours is a large church, and when I arrived, the church administration was already setting up triage support teams. West Palm Beach is a major vacation destination for many New Yorkers, and we anticipated a heavy response. We were right. That day, over one thousand people either came in or called for counseling, advice, and support. Many were unable to reach loved ones, and their desperation was overwhelming. We spent the day talking with them. The next day, I spent 12 hours live on local radio, taking phone calls and counseling people on the air.

For nearly 48 hours on September 11 and 12, I was called upon to perform *under pressure, on demand.* A wise proverb says to prepare for war in a time of peace. When the crisis came on September 11, I didn't have to get ready, because the previous two decades had been my training ground. For years my everyday routine had been to *hope for the best but prepare for the worst.* The call on my entire life is to reach out to and help hurting people. I knew God had a plan. Somehow, I knew I would be directly involved at Ground Zero.

IMPRESSIONS OF A NIGHTMARE

The events of September 11, 2001 kicked into high gear training that I had already been giving to professional athletes, fire and rescue workers, elementary and high school students, and businesses worldwide, including Fortune 100 and 500 companies: *performance under pressure, upon demand through stress utilization.* Later that same day my cell phone began ringing with appeals from the corporate world in New York. One company that called had 3,800 people in the south tower of the World Trade Center and did not yet know how many, if any, had gotten out safely. They were expecting a huge fallout and needed help dealing with the tragedy and its aftermath.

I agreed to come as soon as possible. Once things had settled down somewhat and commercial flights were in the air again, I would be on a plane at the first opportunity. In the meantime, they would have a chance to better assess their situation and determine the status of their employees. As it turned out, my church sponsored me, so I was able to offer my services pro bono. Three weeks after the attacks, I was on my way to Ground Zero.

As I said good-bye to my family and boarded the plane, I wondered what I would see when I arrived in New York City. Everyone on board was somewhat tense and uneasy. We each had undergone a security check more intense and thorough than ever before for a domestic flight. Conversation was polite but strained. Flight attendants were as courteous as usual, but also unusually efficient and businesslike. We never caught even a glimpse of the pilots or flight crew.

I will never forget the view as we flew over Manhattan. The absence of the World Trade Center's gargantuan twin towers was a visual scar on the city's landscape. In their place were 16 square blocks of total devastation. Billowing up from the site was a steady stream of smoldering ash, which continued for months.

On the ground, I noticed something else different: People walking the streets were being kind and courteous toward one another. This was highly unusual, especially in New York. It was as though a spirit of courtesy had taken over the city, creating in people's minds a sense of concern for each other's welfare. Suddenly, everyone mattered. No one was insignificant. Life was something to be valued and cherished, not squandered on pettiness, jealousy, and hatred.

In and around Ground Zero the security was, in a word, intimidating. Security checkpoints were in place every 50 yards or so, and everyone, no matter what their identity or credentials, went through the same security protocols at each checkpoint. There were no exceptions. It was and remains our country's largest crime scene.

No amount of training can prepare you for 16 square blocks of utter destruction. Upon my first entry into Ground

Zero, the scene before me assaulted all my senses. I could hardly believe what I was seeing. Surrounding me was a vast wasteland of smoldering concrete, metal, and ash. Fourteen stories of rubble lay atop each other as though they had been put through a gigantic trash compactor. Massive steel girders were twisted like pretzels. One remaining set of girders stood 40 feet tall in the shape of a cross. Closer toward the epicenter, and atop a 40-story pile of debris, a large American flag, charred, blackened, and badly torn, rippled gently in the wind. The sight of our nation's flag in such a setting moved me to tears, and at that moment I felt so proud to be an American.

Inside Ground Zero, the mood was somber and very quiet as construction workers, firefighters, rescue personnel, police officers, and others worked side by side to uncover fallen colleagues and World Trade Center workers who were entombed when the towers fell. Then there was the smell. A thousand different odors pervaded Ground Zero: gas, dust, smoke, burning cinders–and death. There are times even today when I can close my eyes and still see and smell Ground Zero. It is forever etched in my memory.

CRT AT GROUND ZERO

My first session of CRT–Crisis Response Training–was held on October 4, 2001, in a tiny conference room in the downtown financial district. Over 50 people jammed into a room designed to accommodate 15. Stockbrokers, secretaries, lawyers, couriers, EMS technicians, firefighters, police officers, FEMA workers, computer programmers, doctors; you name it, they were there. For 90 minutes they listened attentively, even desperately, as I shared with them the same thing I had been teaching corporate America for ten years–how to perform *under pressure, on demand.* I gave them the keys to balancing their lives *mentally*, *emotionally*, *spiritually*, and *physically* in the midst of stress and crisis. I stressed the importance of making sure they ate regularly, exercised regularly, and took regular recovery breaks. I took all the research and knowledge from my years working in sports science and athletic performance and applied them to dealing with trauma and chaos–what we could call the *storms of life*.

It was not easy looking into the eyes of grown men and women who were so despondent and fearful that they seemed almost like little children in need of direction. As the training progressed, however, I saw many of them begin to relax as the desperation on their faces slowly melted away. Despair turned into hope and a resolute determination not only to survive but to thrive by never allowing fear to carry the day.

The response to the first training was overwhelming, and one thing quickly led to another. Before long, I was invited to give my training to a law firm whose offices were located at the edge of the 16-block perimeter of Ground Zero. They had no electricity or telephones, and their windows had been blown out. Drapes covered the openings.

Requests for training began pouring in from other companies and organizations as well. Every couple of weeks for the next three months I flew back and forth between Florida and New York, training hundreds of people involved in one way or another with the 9/11 disaster. I conducted multiple training sessions throughout the day, and at night often went into Ground Zero itself, talking with fire and rescue personnel, port authority workers, and others, many of whom were routinely working 24-hour shifts with no breaks. I stressed to them how they needed to make sure they were taking time for personal recovery. Late at night, I would finally get some sleep, then rise early the next morning for another full day of corporate crisis training sessions. That was my life for the last three months of 2001.

As word got around, people lined up to sit through Crisis Response Training. Through the training they received the necessary tools to help them process the trauma as well as useful information to enable them to return to some semblance of normalcy in their everyday lives. Group after group came. It was always a challenge to watch one group leave encouraged and inspired, only to turn around and see the next group coming in with the same blank, hopeless expressions on their faces. Through the tears, however, they focused. Although the visual horror of the time was seared into their collective consciousness, they were able, through training, to process that stress into the power to recover.

During these sessions, in addition to talking, I spent a lot of time listening. People felt they had to tell me their stories in order to process their grief. Except in one respect, no two stories were alike. In every case, the terror and sense of devastation were so real that I could feel it as they spoke. At times it became so overwhelming that I had to take frequent recovery breaks just to vent and process my own emotions. I experienced much the same reaction often during my own visits to Ground Zero. The shock and horror built to such a point that my emotions erupted, but afterwards, I found myself refreshed, recharged and ready to stay on and assist in any way possible. Processing and recovery are essential to health and sanity in dealing with life's storms.

My first return home from Ground Zero was also very emotional. Our dog, Beemer, met me at the door. As I bent over to pet him, I suddenly broke down in a paroxysm of tears. Emotionally, I was torn between being glad to be home and feeling guilty at being alive and able to be with my family after so many other people had died.

After what I saw and felt and experienced that first week in New York, my life will never again be the same. Being at Ground Zero changed me forever. To stand surrounded by absolute devastation in a place where nearly 3,000 human lives had been snuffed out senselessly, a place where over 40 million tons of debris had to be removed, affected me in ways impossible to describe. Watching dedicated rescue workers often wedging themselves into tiny spaces that could easily become fatal for them, simply on the hope—the chance—of finding one more survivor, moved me as nothing else ever has or, perhaps, ever will.

As soon as I got home, I began planning my next trip. I was determined to train, counsel, pray for, and comfort everyone I could. Each visit got a little easier, but the people's stories were still full of grief, horror, and pain. I will never forget the faces of those in the triage training rooms, individuals who were frantically grabbing at anything they could to help them sleep, eat, and return to some kind of peace and equilibrium again.

I carry these memories with me proudly, because they have profoundly affected not only the work I do but also the very life I lead. Every time I kiss Sandy, hug Brandon and Brent, pet Beemer, or train people, I know that I have been blessed with the priceless gift of life. I will never take another moment for granted, nor will I allow idleness to overtake me. Life is too precious.

As precious as life is, it never comes without storms. Since we cannot avoid life's storms, we must learn how to deal with them—how to *navigate* them. September 11, 2001 was a massive storm in the life of our nation, a storm whose effects are still being felt all across the country and, indeed, around the world. Every American was affected, particularly those who lived or worked in and around Ground Zero.

The events of 9/11 changed America and Americans forever. No matter how well we weather the storm, we will never be the same again. On that day we as a nation were introduced to a new level of stress: the awareness that we too are vulnerable to global terrorists who could strike us again at any time and any place. Even as we rise to the challenge and emerge from the rubble of the World Trade Center, steadfast and resolute, the fear, stress, and uncertainty of the days immediately following 9/11 have given way to new ones.

The ongoing struggle against global terrorism, such as America's recent military campaigns in Afghanistan and Iraq, are stark reminders that life storms, even on a global scale, will never go away. One will pass only to be replaced by another. Our survival depends on our success in navigating these storms. Through Crisis Response Training, hundreds of people involved in 9/11 and its aftereffects have learned to process their stress and trauma and to perform under pressure upon demand. They have learned how to navigate the greatest storms ever to hit their lives.

What worked for these hundreds of people at Ground Zero and later will also work for all of us in helping us learn to navigate life's storms.

STRESS EXCELLENCE

Life storms come in many forms: trauma, tragedy, illness, injury, depression, anxiety, financial reversal, divorce, and even the pressures and stress of day-to-day living. With its affinity for "pop" psychology, our modern, sophisticated culture encourages us to deal with these storms by adopting a strategy of avoidance. "Stress management" is a phrase we have heard more and more in recent years. Everywhere we turn we hear that stress is killing us and we need to eliminate it, or at least reduce it to a manageable level. The only problem is, we can't.

Stress is part of life; it is unavoidable. Our efforts to run from pressure, reduce stress, sidestep anxiety and evade the day-to-day battles with worry and apprehension are exercises in futility. No matter how carefully we plan or how hard we try, we will never completely succeed in escaping stressful storms in life. Our only hope of success lies in navigating *through* them. This is very difficult for most of us, for two reasons. First, we have misunderstood the true nature of stress and the role it plays in our lives, and second, we have never been trained to *utilize* it rather than avoid it.

In the 1950s and early 1960s, the ideal husband and father was, in the minds of many, the "strong and silent" type. Unfortunately, in many instances these "strong and silent" men were actually deeply stressed-out and afraid of their emotions. To compensate, they hid their pain and fear behind a veneer of hardness and stoicism. With nowhere else to turn, many of these men tried to deal with their stress through alcohol. Often, the pressure erupted in mental, physical, or sexual abuse and marital infidelity.

These under-pressure-to-perform adults of the '50s became the stressed-out society of the '60s, and passed their dysfunction to their children. For many of the '60s generation, drugs replaced alcohol as the opiate of choice and "free love" replaced traditional marital commitment. Neither generation, however, was taught how to handle the pressures of life, so the dysfunction continued to be transferred from one generation to the next.

So here we are today, at the beginning of a new millennium, in a society that is all stressed-out with nowhere to go. Most of us live well, eat well, dress well, and make good money. We may look good on the outside, but we're stressed-out on the inside and don't know what to do about it. In America alone, stress has cost billions of dollars in lost productivity, poor quality, health problems, and social welfare. It has devastated families and destroyed lives through mental, emotional, and physical illnesses—even death—thus eating away at the very fabric of our society.

For a long time we have struggled in vain to deal successfully with the problem. The main reason for our failure is that we have focused on the wrong thing. We have tried to find ways to *reduce* stress or avoid it as much as possible. This has not worked because *stress is not the problem*. The problem is our inability to process and utilize stress constructively.

Stress is good for us.

Surprised? Although that statement cuts against the grain of almost everything we hear about stress these days, it is true nonetheless. Our bodies are hardwired to handle stress. Just as an ignition sequence converts liquid oxygen and hydrogen into powerful rocket fuel, our physiology is designed to process and convert stress into energy that can enable us to perform at peak efficiency. Properly utilized, stress can propel us toward success in every area of life. Stress is meant to define us, not defeat us; to illuminate us, not eliminate us; to complement our lives, not complicate them.

Pressure, which is another word for stress, squeezes out whatever is inside. Ordinary lumps of coal thrive under pressure, being transformed into precious diamonds. Olives release their valuable oil only when they are put into the press and crushed. The potential for greatness that resides in each of us will be revealed only under pressure. Just as a sponge when squeezed will release whatever liquid it has soaked up, whether dirty or clean, pressure will expose our character, whether good or bad.

We need stress in our lives in order to bring out our highest potential. Pressure is necessary if our talents and skills are to fully emerge. Without pressure, our latent abilities will remain forever hidden and untapped, resulting in a disappointing and unfulfilled life. Pressure can either make us or break us depending upon how we deal with it. Training makes the difference. We will never know who we really are or what we can really do until we pass the "stress test" of *life navigation*. We need stress for success.

Stress for Life Balance

Stress strengthens us. In every zone of life—*mental*, *emotional*, *spiritual*, and *physical*—stress is the stimulus for all growth. If all stress were removed from our lives we would atrophy and eventually die. Studies among senior citizens have demonstrated that if they stop reading, studying, and challenging themselves mentally, their minds begin to atrophy. We need the stress of intellectual challenge to stay healthy mentally. Emotionally, if we fail to heal from a hurt in a personal or professional relationship, we will begin to withdraw. Unwilling to risk being hurt again, we will not expose ourselves and eventually will become insensitive to emotional stimuli. Spiritual atrophy will occur if we lose our connection to our life purpose—why we are on the planet—becoming self-centered and inward-focused as a result. Physically, our bodies will atrophy without exercise, which stresses our muscles and other systems, thereby strengthening them. That's what cardiopulmonary, resistance, and weight training are all about—strengthening the body through stress.

Let's face it, stress happens. We can't avoid it, and since it is so important to our success and progress in life, we shouldn't try. Neither should we attempt to "manage" our stress. Aside from being impossible, "managing" our stress implies limiting our performance. We can't afford to get "stressed out," so we will go only so far and no farther, do only so much and no more. Stress "management" eliminates any possibility of raising the bar of personal performance because it seeks to limit the very thing that makes better performance possible. Instead, we should *embrace* stress, learning to channel it into energy for peak performance and utilizing it to propel us into balance and success in every area of life.

Stress is any opposing force that potentially limits forward progress. It can be anything, any pressure or life storm that hinders our growth, development, or balance in any of the four zones of life–*mental*, *emotional*, *spiritual*, or *physical*. Depending on our perspective, stress may be a liability or an asset. Most of us perceive pressure differently in different arenas of life. What we call *stress* in the corporate world we call *chaos* in the family. In sports, we call it *competition*. The words may be different, but we are talking about the same thing: any opposing force that potentially limits forward progress.

In the corporate world, we fear stress as a killer and try to minimize it. Most of us regard chaos as undesirable in our families and strive for the "ideal" of peace, harmony, and order. We simply want everything to be "normal." Unfortunately, "normal" is a relative term. People commonly ask me to define "normal," and my usual reply is that God is the only normal thing in the universe and everyone else is simply at different levels of strange.

Because we have a special-needs son, my own family would not meet most people's idea of "normal," but we have come to grips with the painful reality that this is the hand we have been dealt. In the game of life, success comes not in wishing we had a different hand to play, but in how well we play the hand we have. Navigating life's storms means learning to use the stress and chaos that come our way to strike a balance at every level. Life happens, and it isn't always fair. How we *respond* to life spells the difference between success and failure.

We fear stress in the workplace and chaos at home because that is how our society has programmed us. Fear arises from an absence of peace or from a misaligned or imbalanced mind/body state, and is itself a form of stress. Our response to fear determines in large measure the course of our lives. It can be either a stumbling block or a stepping-stone. Fear is one of the most significant factors that impedes our forward progress and prevents us from pursuing excellence and all that life has to offer. At the same time, we can learn to master fear, to harness it and use it to navigate ourselves toward successful performance. It all depends on how we *position* it.

Positioning our fear has a lot to do with how our minds translate beliefs into pictures, a process known as *info-imaging*. In infoimaging, specific information is connected in our minds with a unique image, which can be recalled later as needed. We can learn to associate our fears with a specific mental image that will distance us emotionally from them, thus defusing their destructive and self-limiting effects.

Mastering our fear requires that we have in us an ingredient that positions us to be protected for the unexpected—the unknown. *We* are the *known* quantity in every unknown situation we face; *we* are the "*x*" factor in fear's equation. Once we train to balance ourselves *mentally*, *emotionally*, *spiritually*, and *physically*, no storm that comes against us will be able to carry the day. *A life that is in balance is storm-proof.*

THRIVING UNDER PRESSURE

This is why we need to learn how to look at stress and chaos the same way athletes view competition. We are programmed to look at stress as something negative to be feared and avoided. In sports, stress comes in the form of competition. Athletes, however, do not fear competition; they *live* for it. Olympic athletes train rigorously for years for one opportunity to measure themselves against the world's best in their event. Elite performers in any field are always striving to improve, always looking for opportunities to raise the bar and challenge their best to become even better.

Consider professional athletes, particularly top-of-the-line players such as Tiger Woods, Michael Jordan, Martina Navratilova, Wayne Gretsky, Jackie Joyner-Kersee, or Barry Bonds. If we were to ask them whether they feared competition, they would say something like, "Of course not. I live to compete. As a matter of fact, the better the competition, the better I get."

Elite performers like these have trained to love competition, because they know that competition is not their problem. Competition is a magnifying glass to showcase their talent and skill and their ability to perform *under pressure, on demand*. In an NBA playoff with seconds to go and one point under, why will Michael Jordan be given the ball? During sudden death play for the NHL championship, why will Wayne Gretsky get the puck? The answer is simple: Both men are *proven* talents *under pressure, on demand*.

Great athletes embrace the challenge of pitting their skills against others. They *thrive* under the pressure of competition. That is what separates the elite from the average. Many people struggle simply to *survive* under pressure. Many others manage to *function* under pressure, to keep things going at least to a minimal degree. Few people, however, learn to *thrive* under pressure. Those who do have learned to regard pressure not as a liability but as an asset, not as an adversary but as an ally.

Few of us develop this kind of mind-set naturally. We must learn it through training that helps us see that life pressure is normal, and teaches us to have a proactive focus that predisposes and positions us toward excellence.

I recall once watching a television program on the life of NBA great Earvin "Magic" Johnson. The star shared that as a youngster he would play basketball alone in his back yard, imagining that he was in the NBA finals, and calling the play-by-play in his mind as he shot baskets. Typically, he would imagine something like:

It's the final game of the championship, with ten seconds to go. The home team is down by one; they need one basket to win. They give it to Johnson; he dribbles left, stops at the top of the key. Five seconds; he shakes, he bakes. Three seconds; he fakes out his man. Two seconds; he leaps. One second; he shoots–nothing but the bottom of the net! The buzzer sounds, the game is over, the home team wins, Johnson is the hero!

This kind of self-imposed training (info-imaging) at an early age instilled in "Magic" Johnson a hunger for the pressure of competition, not a fear of it. He embraced that pressure and went on to one of the most celebrated and outstanding careers in NBA history. Through training, he was able to rise to the occasion and perform *under pressure, on demand* with consistent and predictable results.

Stress and Recovery

The first key to positioning ourselves for consistent excellence of performance under pressure is to understand that stress is not the problem. Properly utilized, stress is healthy and an asset in seeking high quality performance in any area of life. If we want to walk among the elite, we must be able to "suck it up" and say, "Bring on the stress; I love it. I thrive on it. It helps me become better at what I do."

If stress is not the problem, what is? The problem is *insufficient periodic recovery*. In other words, we all need a balanced work-rest cycle that runs on 90-minute intervals, because that is how we are wired. Our physiology is designed for a regular 90-minute oscillatory cycle of stress-recovery, stress-recovery, stress-recovery throughout the day. Just like an oscillating fan, we are at our best and most effective when we keep moving. Anything that is still for too long becomes stagnant and begins to die. *Unrelieved* stress is dangerous, but quick oscillatory recovery at regular intervals enables us to process stress in healthy ways that lead to enhanced performance.

Physiological studies clearly demonstrate that 90 minutes is the optimal peak performance window; two hours is the ceiling. It does not matter what we are doing, whether we are working or playing, active or inactive. Without recovery, our *mental*, *emotional*, *spiritual*, and *physical* acuities drop dramatically after two hours. We need brief, periodic breaks—even just a simple change of activity or focus—in order to restore our sharpness.

This is not "pop" psychology or the latest fad, but the result of years of study in sports and behavioral sciences. Football games, basketball games, and other athletic contests are divided by periodic breaks—time-outs, quarters, halftime, etc.—and with good reason. Running at such high levels without stopping for periodic recovery would deplete energy so quickly that even the best players would drop dead.

In the corporate and family worlds people *are* dropping dead *mentally*, *emotionally*, *spiritually*, and *physically*, and we wonder why. It's as if we don't understand why people cannot run at Mach 2 with their hair on fire seven days a week. No one can; it's not in our wiring. For optimal health and peak performance on an ongoing basis, we must have regular, consistent periods of recovery.

Lack of recovery is the main reason so many of us have trouble coping with the demands of today's fast-paced living. Although we are *wired* for success, many of us are *programmed* for failure. Society has programmed us to believe that more and faster are always better, but that is not true. We *can* handle more, we *can* raise the bar and continue to raise it, but we *must* take regular breaks for recovery. God took a break after creating the world, not because He needed it but because He knew *we* would need it. He designed us for success and performance excellence, but He also designed us to operate on 90-minute oscillatory cycles of stress and recovery.

This cycle of stress and recovery is true for everyone, not just athletes. Regular periodic recovery is critical for consistently performing well *under pressure, on demand* on a continuing basis. Consider Broadway performers, for example. They operate at a level of consistency and excellence that is simply amazing. Day in and day out it's the same. No matter how many times they have performed a role, each performance will move the audience as if it is the very first one. One actress in the hit musical *Cats* appeared six days a week for 13 years. How do they do this? How do they stay so fresh and so good day after day and week after week without losing their edge? First, they have learned through training how to handle the stress of such a demanding schedule, and second, they have learned how to recover.

Much of the corporate world has been slow to learn this. Until recent years, talk of a work/rest cycle was little more than a joke in corporate circles. The prevailing attitude said that we *work* on the job and *rest* at home. Working hard and steadily through the day is expected and required; anything less is unacceptable. We put in our eight or ten hours at the office then "recover" when we go home. Unless we find a way to recover regularly throughout the day–to navigate the storm of pressure–the first two hours are work, while the rest is struggle.

People who have learned to listen to their body, to read its signals, and respond accordingly have discovered that they have more energy over a longer sustained period of time and consistently perform at a higher level of efficiency and excellence than they did before. Average people usually do not figure this out because they have become too programmed by society's mantra that says, "Keep working. More is better. The longer you work, the tougher you are." That's crazy. It's like trying to hold our hand over our head for an hour. We can't do it. The blood rushes out of it, gravity takes over, and eventually it drops. Every day we have to fight the "gravity" of bad programming in our lives, our work, and families. Stress will always be there, so if we are not recovering regularly, we are fighting a losing battle against something that is never going to change.

The only thing that separates clean, healthy water from stagnant, infected water is movement. Running water is always cleaner than still water because in running water bacteria have less opportunity to grow. A stream has purer water than a pond because the flow of water over the rocks in the streambed has a cleansing effect. The Dead Sea is dead because it has no outlet. With nowhere to go, its water stagnates and slowly evaporates, building up an alkali level so high that virtually nothing can live there.

Our bodies are the same way. If we stop moving we die *mentally*, *emotionally*, *spiritually*, and *physically*. We have to keep moving. That's why our mind is always active, why our heart keeps beating and our blood keeps flowing. That's why our lungs keep inspiring and expiring oxygen. We have to keep moving to keep living.

A Balancing Act

There is an area of the brain called the *amygdala*, whose primary function is processing our emotional experiences and helping us modulate the difference between fiction and reality. This is what we call *perception*. Part of the limbic system of the brain, which is associated with emotion and motivation, the *amygdala* assists us in rational thinking so that our perception will line up with reality. Watching a scary movie might lead us to a perception that makes us too afraid to fall asleep. Rational thinking helps restore the balance between our perception and reality as we tell ourselves, "It's all right, it's not real. It's only a movie."

How we perceive and respond to the world around us depends upon how well we understand a concept that I call the 90/10 rule. This rule is based on the fact that 100 percent of reality is shaped by 90 percent of pure old perception. We often find life so frustrating because so many of us spend 90 percent of our time trying to change the 10 percent of reality that will never change. Instead, we should use the 90 percent that *can* change to strengthen us in dealing with the 10 percent that is constant. The biggest challenge is learning how to correctly identify what falls into that 10 percent category.

Here's an example. If I want to watch a sunrise, I must plan in accordance with unchanging realities. Let's say I get up early one morning, eat breakfast, and go outside and settle myself into a lawn chair to wait for my sunrise. Then, to my dismay, the sun comes up over my shoulder. No matter how much I may desire it or how many times I try, I will never see a sunrise by facing the west. My own perceptions aside, if I want to see the sunrise, I must adjust my plans to conform to the 10 percent rule of the solar system that says that the rising of the sun in the *eastern* sky is an unchanging reality.

Perception and focus are closely related. Perception is how we *see* reality, whether true or false; focus is directing our attention to a particular thing to the exclusion of any other distractions. Our perception guides and aims our focus. How we perceive the daily pressures of life determines where we place our focus, and that decision will either empower or cripple us in reaching for our true potential. Once our perception and focus line up with reality, we can live life on different terms.

As with fear, balancing life is a perceptual problem. Success depends on whether or not our perceptions are based on true reality. One misconception that many people have is that balance in life is an end in itself. This is not so. Life balance is not a destination as much as it is a *journey*. When we learn to achieve balance between the *mental*, *emotional*, *spiritual*, and *physical* aspects of our being, governed by prescribed values and routines, we will come to a place of heightened concentration, a singular focus where everything works together for optimum performance. This is what athletes call being "in the zone."

The "zone" is the measure of difference between mediocrity and excellence. We all have great days once in a while, but getting into the "zone" consistently is a matter of training and alignment. *Consistent* performance excellence can be summoned on demand only through specific training to produce *mental, emotional, spiritual,* and *physical* alignment for life toughness.

In this journey of life and work, balance and routines go hand in hand. Show me your routines and I will show you the building blocks of success. Show me the lack of routines and I will show you an accident waiting to happen. This is why in pressure situations the coach will not look to the end of the bench for the mediocre player but will go to the proven performer. As a matter of fact, it is the elite players who will be in the coach's face saying, "Give me the ball! Let me win the game!" They get depressed when they are *not* called upon in pressure situations because those are the moments they live for, the moments they have worked and trained for. Those are the moments when they *thrive.*

Reaching and maintaining elite status in any area can be achieved only through a *daily* balancing routine where we focus our mental, emotional, spiritual, and physical quadrants each morning. This process is called *alignment,* and it serves to keep us focused on the center of our purpose. Alignment prepares us for anything and everything that we may encounter throughout the day.

Stressology, or the study of performance under pressure, is the result of 20 years of comprehensive, qualitative, and controlled study in the fields of medicine, science, sports, neurochemistry, psychology, and military and special forces training, along with thousands of hours of research. It is not "pop" psychology, a fad, or a passing trend, but a revolutionary discipline that produces measurable and quantifiable results. Through this training we can learn to navigate the storms of life and perform at peak levels *mentally, emotionally, spiritually,* and *physically, under pressure, on demand.*

Chapter Two

Life Navigation

The privilege of a life is being who you are.

–Joseph Campbell

When I was a boy, my mother often used a pressure cooker to prepare the meals for our family. She would throw in a batch of pinto beans, add some water, turn the fire on under the pot, and then lock down the lid with its special spigot for releasing the steam. Heat combined with pressure caused the food to cook faster, but the steam that built up inside the pot needed to be released periodically.

I remember one day walking into the kitchen, where the pot's steam spigot was hissing, and asking my mother, "What will happen if you don't let off the steam?"

"The pot will explode," she answered.

Life is a lot like a pressure cooker. Stress applies heat, the pressure builds up, and unless we find a consistent way to "let off steam," we will explode. Unless we learn how to recover, the continuing pressures of life will cause everything–relationships, job opportunities, our personal dreams, goals, and ambitions–to blow up in our faces.

That is exactly what is happening all across the country. Professionals, laborers, business executives, teachers, police officers, firefighters, rescue workers—people from every walk of life—are "blowing up" because they do not know how to recover from stress properly and periodically or how to "debrief" after a crisis or an especially traumatic event. This is why specific training in life navigation is so important. The value of training lies not only in teaching us how to perform our jobs better and to rise to the occasion day after day, but also in showing us what to do afterwards—teaching us how to deal with the aftermath of the events, both big and small, that occur in our lives.

Public safety personnel such as police officers, firefighters, and rescue workers are good examples. These people are specially trained to perform under pressure day after day, whether investigating crimes, responding to emergencies, fighting fires, rendering emergency medical assistance or providing disaster relief. Usually, they are the first on the scene of an accident. Every day they deal with crises up close and personal, in what is called *first response, high clean up*.

Unfortunately, many of these well-trained and highly motivated individuals have never been taught how to deal with the fallout of what they see, hear, and smell every day. They know how to handle the crisis at hand, but often have no clue on how to debrief—how to process the stress of that crisis—or even that they *need* to debrief.

No matter how horrific or tragic an event may be, the prevailing attitude of police, fire, rescue, or other first responders quite often is, "I'm tough. I'm trained to handle this. I don't need stress debriefing." Unfortunately, this attitude is culturally ingrained and difficult to dislodge. As a result, many of these workers who have been through a traumatic experience end up whittling away at their lives.

Their families disintegrate and they lose touch with reality, all because they did not debrief or properly process their stress.

SPECIAL FORCES/LIFE TRAINING

Whether we are dealing with crisis or trauma or simply pursuing our normal day-to-day activities, the challenge is the same: processing and utilizing the stress in our lives to propel us to consistent excellence and peak performance. In either case the key to success is training.

Training does not merely *impart* skill but rather identifies and develops those talents and abilities that are already present. Consider the training of military Special Forces, for example. Special Forces training is specifically designed to push people to the breaking limit quickly in order to weed out those who cannot survive from those who can. It includes the process of breaking down and rebuilding trainees' *mental*, *emotional*, *spiritual*, and *physical* capacities in a highly controlled life navigational environment.

My work studying the effects and utilization of stress brought me in contact with an admiral who was a Navy SEAL and who trained Navy SEALs for over a decade. SEAL training is a brutal 26-week regimen with a 70-percent dropout rate. I asked this admiral why the training was so tough. He replied that they elevated the stress level so high in order to quickly separate out the ones who could not handle it, and return them to their former units. Those who remained—those who were able to dig down deeply enough to find something within themselves that enabled them to keep pushing and not to give up—were then ready to be trained as SEALs.

The first part of SEAL training is sheer survival. It forces each trainee to face the question, "Are you tough enough?" and quickly distinguishes those who have what it takes from those who do not. SEAL training does not *impart* the necessary toughness, but brings it out in those who already possess it, (even if they are not aware of it at first), and then helps them develop that toughness to peak efficiency and readiness.

While most people tend to view tragedy, chaos, stress, and pressure as things to be avoided, the opposite is true in the military. Military training, and Special Forces training in particular, does not protect participants from fear, pain, pressure, or uncertainty, but instead exposes them to the most extreme conditions possible in order to strengthen their *mental*, *emotional*, *spiritual*, and *physical* capacities.

Life experience and specific toughness training can empower most people to go far beyond their original assessment of logical boundaries and human potential. The tough things in life can either propel us toward excellence or cause us to surrender in defeat. Unfortunately, the United States has birthed several generations of people who, believing that life pressures will limit health and happiness, seek to avoid pain and suffering at all costs. In fact, the opposite is true: Removing pressure from a person's mind/body capacities will result in weakness, increased illness, confusion, mood swings, atrophy, and even death. Remember that pressure (stress) is nothing more than an opposing force that potentially limits forward progress. Stress adds challenge and flavor to life. We should see challenges not as something to fear, but as training opportunities to equip us for life excellence.

Everybody is born with a measure of talent and skill in some area or another, but it is training that will make the difference between mediocrity and excellence in performance. Talent is important, but by itself is rarely enough. To be gifted is one thing, but to be gifted *and* good is another, and demands a disciplined approach for achieving life excellence.

Training helps someone become better at what he or she is *already* talented at. In sports, a coach does not *give* an athlete talent; they take existing talent and improve it.

A certain degree of natural talent is necessary for any athlete to make the team. The coach's responsibility is to help those athletes develop their talent and to make sure that they each are positioned on the team where they can perform at their highest level. A good coach will not switch an excellent defensive player to offense unless he has reason to believe that offense is where that athlete's true talent lies.

Training is about helping people identify where they are at their best and then teaching them how to "plug in"—to align themselves with what they do well. Tapping into talent and skill *under pressure, on demand* requires that all individual capacities—*mental, emotional, spiritual,* and *physical*—come together in a unique and synergistic alignment that will produce consistent peak performance. This is true whether we are talking about athletics, the arts, job performance, or navigating the storms of life.

HURRICANE AT HOME

For my wife, Sandy, and me, life navigation training was no luxury. It was critical to our survival. If life storms come to everyone, then the storm that hit our home early in our marriage arrived with hurricane force that has never abated. Had we not learned to navigate in the midst of it, that storm would have destroyed us.

When our eldest son, Brandon, was born, we were living in Anchorage, Alaska with an orderly life plan laid out before us. Brandon's arrival changed all that. Like any other expectant parent, I found the prospect of becoming a first-time father both exciting and challenging. Little did I realize just *how* challenging raising Brandon would be. He arrived seemingly with a warning label that said, "Beware of sleep deprivation!" Until then, nighttime in our home was something to enjoy. With Brandon's birth, nightlife took on a whole new meaning.

I remember how proud I was as a father when Brandon was born. He was such a precious little guy, and I looked forward to doing so many things with him, to experiencing everything imaginable for a father with his son. At the time I had no idea how much of a role model and hero Brandon would become for me. I am convinced that Brandon was sent to our family in order for me to experience for myself, and then share with the world, how important it is to enjoy and maximize life every moment of every day. Brandon's particular life challenges reshaped my thinking about everything and everyone around me.

At 12 months of age, Brandon developed an ongoing digestion problem that caused all of us some grief. When the doctors in Anchorage were unable to identify Brandon's problem, we traveled to the "Lower 48" for more help. After an extended stay in a children's hospital, we were informed that Brandon was suffering from some sort of brain disorder, a condition so rare that it could not be linked with any other case in the United States. With no clear prognosis or even a baseline for understanding what was happening to Brandon, the doctors could tell us little more than that recovery was unlikely and that he probably would not live very long.

One concerned and puzzled doctor summed it up when he said to us, "Mr. and Mrs. Lyles, we don't know what is wrong with your son, but we do know that his brain is dying." It was then that Sandy and I began to realize that our lives would never again be the same. Brandon developed seizures and muscle spasms that created a continuous life storm for us like nothing we had ever experienced before. The knowledge that I would never hear my son say, " I love you," or "Play ball with me," was almost more than I could bear. The pain in his tortured little body increased daily, so that he was unable to sleep for more than a few hours at a time. Because Brandon could not sleep through the night, neither could Sandy and I. Sleep deprivation became the *norm* in our home.

Because of his multiple problems and physical discomfort, Brandon required constant care. Sandy and I began trading off in three-hour shifts through the night with him, mixing medicines and rolling him regularly to help alleviate his pain. I would sit with him until the sun came up to remind me that I had just survived another 24 hours. Brandon continued to decline daily while we did everything possible to ease his suffering. Sometimes I wondered if facing my own death wouldn't be easier than watching Brandon's slow and painful decline. Although upset and confused, Sandy and I continued to hold onto each other and waited every day for either a miracle or Brandon's anticipated death.

Another tough issue for us was the seemingly endless rounds of medical tests and hospital visits. Sandy's strong love and gentleness with Brandon made it possible for me to be the "bad guy," assisting the doctors by holding Brandon down for the many painful procedures they needed to perform in an effort to identify the mysterious disease that was robbing our son of life. I will never forget the pain in his eyes as I tried to console him through those terrible times. Many times, if we learn to view our circumstances in the right light, the most difficult situations can become the proving ground where we learn our most important lessons. Through all of this, Brandon and I bonded in a very special way that is difficult to explain. We endured so much pain together—his physical, and mine emotional—that we became true soul mates.

The first couple of years after the onset of Brandon's illness were horrendous for us. We could hardly believe what the doctors were telling us about our son. Complications were one thing, but a terminal illness with no diagnosis or identifiable cause to be found anywhere in the world? That news was almost unbearable for us. I can still remember the pain in my heart and the confusion in my head. How could this happen to us? We had tried to live right and believed that God understood where we were. Why was Brandon sick? Why couldn't the doctors diagnose and treat his illness? There were so many questions, but so few answers. The days turned into weeks and the weeks, months, and we were still trying to figure out what to do next and how to cope with the curveball life had thrown us.

Turning Point

I quickly began to hate the storm that had hit our house and never gave us any relief. We prayed for healing, we questioned the doctors frequently, we continued in daily therapy, we asked for help everywhere we could until we burned out everyone around us. Our faith in God grew stronger even as our bodies and minds grew more tired. By the time two years had passed, we were wearing thin and running out of friends and family who could help us weather the storm of "Hurricane Brandon." It became clear that no matter how long Brandon lived he would never be able to sit up on his own, crawl, walk, feed himself, or control his bodily functions.

When Brandon was three years old, orthopedists told us that we needed to fit him for a special wheelchair. Until that time, Brandon was so small we carried him in a baby carrier. As he grew, however, he would need the special support of a fitted wheelchair because his muscles could not support him properly and he would develop spine and hip problems and other issues. Getting him fitted was a pretty painless process. We took him in and made sure he sat correctly while a clay mold was made, from which a contoured seating device was poured. It was a perfect fit. Now Brandon could feel supported, secure, and comfortable.

Our first venture into public with Brandon in his wheelchair was a real eye-opener for me, a turning point in my life because I was brought face-to-face with myself. We took Brandon to the mall. Brandon loved going to the mall. Before, we had always been able to "cheat" with him. Since he was so small that we carried him in a baby carrier, no one else knew that he was a special needs child. With his wheelchair, however, we could not hide him any longer.

Here we were, walking into the mall, with Brandon in his chair. Brandon's wheelchair was a kind of freaky-looking device, bright neon blue with different devices screwed into it, but it worked, and Brandon was comfortable. He felt good in his chair because he was strapped in and secure, and could sit up. He also was very glad to be at the mall. As we walked in, Brandon had his arms up and was making all sorts of weird noises and inarticulate cries, often at the top of his voice. He was happy.

I was pushing the wheelchair with my head down, crying out silently to God and asking "Why?" In my heart I was saying, "Brandon, come on man, chill out! It's bad enough that you're in this neon blue wheelchair, but you're screaming at the top of your lungs, and all these people are looking at me." Right then it hit me. God spoke in my heart and said, "You are more handicapped than he is. Brandon is okay with who he is, but you are not." I was the one with the greater disability because Brandon was secure and satisfied, while I was trying to fix his condition so that *I* could feel better. That moment of revelation changed my life.

Stopping, I knelt in front of Brandon, apologized to him, and promised him that I would never be ashamed of him again. That was when my healing really began to take place. It had taken two years of fear, frustration, and worry to get there, but that moment in the mall was the doorway out of the pit. I realized that this storm in my life was not leaving any time soon, and if I didn't learn to navigate better, I was in danger of losing everything and everyone important to me.

One thing was suddenly clear to me: For Sandy and me, this life circumstance with Brandon would either make us stronger or it would kill us even before Brandon had a chance to die. No one we knew could understand our situation, much less help relieve the pain of our everyday life. Sandy was growing more tired each day and I was so worn-out that I could not think clearly enough to see what all of this was doing to her. Since that day, however, we have learned to rely on each other and on God, because no one else can truly relate to our circumstances. It is good to have no idea what tomorrow holds, because if we did, we would run for the shelter of yesterday.

At the time of this writing, Brandon is 18 years old, but looks like he is five. He is only 48 inches tall, and it is hard to find hats that fit him because his head is still the size of an infant's. Yet, Brandon continues to enjoy life, even through daily struggles, locked in a body where he cannot communicate verbally, balance himself without the bracing of his wheelchair, feed himself, or control his bodily functions.

The only things that pulled us through those painful first years of fear and shock were our faith in God and trust in His promises. Today more than ever before, I realize how important every single day can be. I used to live with the constant awareness that death could visit our family at any moment. Now, because of Brandon's broken body and uncertain future, I live each day to the fullest with a better understanding of my life purpose. I have learned so much from Brandon. What began as the shock and disappointment of my life turned into the opportunity of a lifetime. Where I am today is the result of God's purpose for Brandon in teaching me how to maximize daily pressure through life navigation training.

My point is this: There is no life storm so severe or so prolonged that you cannot learn to navigate through it. For 17 years Sandy and I have navigated a storm that continues to challenge us at every turn. If *we* can do it, *anyone* can do it.

ALIGNMENT IS CRITICAL

When our family first moved to south Florida, we received a demonstration right away of how storms can change our lives. We had barely arrived—our household goods were still in boxes—before I hopped on an airplane and flew to another city. A day and a half later, Hurricane Irene hit. All our plans had to be put on hold temporarily because we had not had time to prepare before the storm arrived.

Sometimes in life we are not as prepared as we think we are, and don't really find out until a storm comes. Since we can't avoid life storms, we must learn how to weather them, and that requires life toughness. Part of developing life toughness is learning a process for navigating the storms. This involves, among other things, understanding our *mission critical data,* those things that are absolutely essential for us to know and do if we are to achieve success.

Navigating life storms can be likened to flying an aircraft. In spite of sophisticated automatic piloting systems, airplanes cannot fly themselves. Experienced and knowledgeable pilots are necessary for taxiing on and off the runway, for takeoffs and landings, and for controlling the operation of the aircraft at all times. In the same way, we cannot simply breeze through life on automatic pilot. We may have our rituals, routines, and habits, but life happens in the midst of it all, and life does not always play by our rules.

Whether flying a plane or dealing with life, there are certain critical systems we must understand. A pilot needs to know his flight plan, his instrument gauges, his radar system, and his vehicle, or transport device, which is the aircraft itself. In life these equate to the *mental*, *emotional*, *spiritual*, and *physical* zones, respectively.

Mental acuity is the "flight plan" in our lives, the *mission critical data* that we have to *know* in order to navigate successfully. The first thing we need to know about our flight plan is that we've got to align ourselves. Alignment is critical. We must make sure that everything is "checked off" before we take off.

Pilots sitting in the cockpit of an airplane have a consistent routine of preflight checks that they go through before every departure. It doesn't matter how many times they have done it before or how many flights they will make on a given day, the procedure is always the same. They will spend 45 minutes to an hour looking at the same book and checking off the same items every time they board an aircraft: wipers, check; oil, check; fuel, check; etc. They may know that checklist forward and backward, but they never rely on their memory. Instead, they read through it line by line by line by line. Why? If they don't, and later make a mistake, someone will probably die, perhaps an entire aircraft full of people.

This is called a zero tolerance work environment: Make a mistake and someone dies. Pilots don't settle for "close"; they make sure. In a zero tolerance environment, excellence becomes the *minimum* acceptable standard. Otherwise, the casualties may be high.

At one time I had a chance to be exposed to the training environment of the Blue Angels, the aerobatics and aerial demonstration team of the United States Navy, studying how they prepared for their job. Before every flight, before ever going onto the tarmac, they reviewed an extensive checklist of everything they were going to do in the air. Seated around a table, the team would visualize and go through every step of every maneuver, checking all the gauges and instruments, checking everything around them, knowing who was in the protocol of line, who's commanding officer, who's first flight, who's second flight, who's third flight, and so on.

This elite team of military pilots would go through the entire flight plan, reviewing and practicing every move. "Okay, we're doing 350 miles per hour, we're 600 feet above the ground. Plane one, you're ready; mark, swing right; plane two; plane three." It took them as long to go through the procedure on the ground as it did to fly the maneuvers in the air. They were getting themselves aligned *mentally*, *emotionally*, *spiritually*, and *physically*. Why? If they did not, and made a mistake at 350 miles per hour doing 4 Gs, they would die and most likely take someone else with them, who was sitting right next to them at the table. Theirs is a zero tolerance environment with no margin for error. Failure is not an option. Alignment is critical.

ALIGNMENT IS NOT AUTOMATIC

Alignment is the daily process of understanding our *mission critical data*, recognizing what is most important for us *mentally*, *emotionally*, *spiritually*, and *physically* if we are to navigate life successfully today. This alignment is critical if we are to work consistently at our highest optimal level of peak performance. As critical as it is, however, alignment is not automatic. It will not happen unless we plan for it and, even more importantly, unless we train to do it.

This alignment or balancing of our mental, emotional, spiritual, and physical acuities is what athletes refer to as being "in the zone." Athletes who are in the zone have all their faculties in these four areas synchronized and focused on the task at hand: competing at their very best and performing at their optimal level. Because their mental, emotional, spiritual, and physical acuities are aligned and working in harmony, they play better, recover from mistakes or setbacks more quickly, and are less affected by distractions.

For athletes, alignment begins long before the game. In the locker room and even before, they will listen to music, or focus their minds on the upcoming contest. They will think about everything that could go wrong as well as all the things that could go right, and about what to do to minimize the first and maximize the second. They will study their opponent very carefully and rehearse in their minds what they need to do to counteract his strategy.

Whether we are athletes, military, police, firefighters, rescue personnel, health care professionals, business executives, office or factory workers–no matter what our career or occupation–we must learn to use what the military calls *situational awareness*, a process for bringing into clear focus everything that is wrong in a specific situation in order to determine how to make it right. Situational awareness helps us pay attention to all the things around us that affect our lives *mentally*, *emotionally*, *spiritually*, and *physically*, so that we can accomplish the alignment that will make us effective in the midst of chaos, competition, tragedy, or other stresses on a regular and daily basis.

What usually happens with most of us, however, is that we wake up in the morning with little or no real awareness of the situation around us and, if we think about alignment at all, assume that these four zones in our lives will somehow come into alignment automatically. It does not happen that way. Scientific studies have revealed that while one or two of those things will get us out of bed, the others will follow because it is a cybernetic loop. As a result of that looping system, whatever your strong suit is on any given day will dominate the others. That would be considered an average day.

Perhaps you wake up feeling great physically and jump out of bed ready to go. Your physical energy may carry you through the day, but what if you have trouble focusing on your job because your mental processes that day can't keep up with your physical acuity?

An optimal day requires that all four zones–*mental, emotional, spiritual,* and *physical*–be brought into equal alignment so they can work together in harmony and pull together like a well-matched team of horses. Making this alignment is neither automatic nor always easy, but it can be learned through *training.*

How do police officers, firefighters, or rescue workers prepare themselves for that emergency call at 2:00 a.m.? *Training.* What makes a Navy SEAL able to jump out of a helicopter over the water after being awakened in the middle of the night, and swim to shore with 40-50 pounds of equipment, even when he doesn't "feel" like it? What makes him able to crawl around on the beach for hours, neutralizing land mines before the Marines arrive in the morning to do their job? *Training.*

Training is important because it teaches us how to do what we need to do regardless of the situation. We learn how to respond consistently under pressure without thinking about it; our response becomes second nature. If we have to *think* about what to do when we are *under pressure*, we won't do it. On the other hand, if we have trained in advance to align ourselves *mentally*, *emotionally*, *spiritually*, and *physically*, when the pressure comes, that training will trigger itself and we will respond with peak performance. We will be operating "in the zone" no matter what the situation.

Performance Is the Bottom Line

Alignment directly influences daily performance. Our ability to align ourselves *mentally*, *emotionally*, *spiritually*, and *physically* will determine how well we perform on a day-to-day basis. Performance is the bottom line in navigating the storms of life, whether we are talking about military operations, athletic competition, corporate and occupational stress, family chaos, or any other kinds of pressure.

How does this four-way alignment play out in reality? What are its benefits? Consider the corporate world, for example. *Mentally*, if workers think more clearly throughout the day, they will make fewer mistakes. If they are in tune with themselves *emotionally*, they won't spend time trashing those around them or sabotaging each other over work-related issues. *Spiritually*, if they understand their purpose–if they know why they punch in every day–they will not walk around aimlessly misusing corporate time. If they are aligned *physically*, they will look better, feel better, and have more energy to give on the job so they can make more money while they are on the clock. *Alignment directly influences daily performance.*

In order to *improve* our performance, we must be able to *measure* our performance. At the end of the day we should be able to ask, "How did I do?" and have a measurable standard to apply in answering. Usually, this is easiest to do in the corporate world because instruments are in place to measure progress. Businesses routinely use annual performance evaluations, quotas, commissions, and other such measurement tools to determine who gets promoted, who gets a raise, who gets an award, and who does not.

When it comes to personal life and relationships, however, most people never measure their own performance. Quite often, they don't know how. On the job, if we fail to perform according to established standards, we will be fired. Who will "fire" us from our personal lives if we don't take care of ourselves? No one. We have to keep score or we will never know whether or not we are winning. Most people do not win because they do not keep score. They may be winning and never even know it.

The problem we run into is that we are wired one way and programmed another. Our programming tells us that it is "normal" on any given day for one acuity–*mental*, *emotional*, *spiritual*, or *physical*–to get us out of bed in the morning and drive us through the day while the other three scramble to catch up. One day I might wake up so on track *emotionally* that I feel like I can save the world. At the same time, I may be so distracted *mentally* because I feel so good that I don't know who to save first. A deep sense of spiritual purpose one day may be derailed by a body wracked with illness, pain, or fatigue. With our *mental*, *emotional*, *spiritual*, and *physical* acuities out of balance, we never know from one day to the next which one will govern. Life then becomes a daily crapshoot, with our performance level completely unpredictable.

In truth, however, we are hardwired in such a way that these four zones are inseparably interconnected. One of the keys to performance *under pressure, on demand* is learning to align these capacities in a way that acknowledges their interconnectedness. Whatever performance level we are seeking, in whatever area, we need a reliable system to help us align our *mental, emotional, spiritual,* and *physical* zones so that they hit the bull's-eye simultaneously, enabling us to perform at our optimal level. Research and work in sports science on how people focus brought about such a system that is measurable, predictable, and reproducible.

Take a Daily Inventory

Alignment means arriving at a *situational awareness* of the things around us, both large and small, that influence our *mental, emotional, spiritual,* and *physical* zones at any given time. The fastest way to accomplish this is by taking a simple daily inventory; running through a daily checklist just as a pilot does before takeoff. I'm not talking about a great deal of time here—only two to five minutes a day. Morning is the best time because the purpose of the inventory is to align ourselves in all four areas so that we can be at our peak for the day ahead. This brief inventory gives us a chance to consider and remind ourselves of all the little details we need to take stock of throughout the day.

The average person walks through life without giving attention to detail. They don't remember peoples' names when they meet them, or what time of day it was when something occurred. They don't pay attention *throughout* the day because they don't *begin* their day paying attention. That's a lot like jumping out of an airplane and *then* checking to see if you have your parachute.

Rarely do we succeed accidentally. Once in a while, we may luck onto something and have a great day. Consistent success cannot depend on luck. Winston Churchill said, "Success is never final." That's a powerful statement that means we cannot rest on our laurels. We have to succeed over and over and over again. We have to *plan* for success over and over and over again. Daily alignment of our four zones is a critical part of that plan.

Basically, alignment is a pretty simple process. Take a few minutes every morning to assess where you are *mentally*, *emotionally*, *spiritually*, and *physically*. One way is to rate yourself in each area from 1-10, with 1 being low and 10 high. Ask yourself some probing questions.

Mentally. "Where am I right now mentally? When I wake up, am I focused, or am I distracted? What am I focused on? What do I need to know today? If I feel distracted, what can I eliminate so that I won't be distracted? What's most important for me to remember today? How can I stay focused? Do I need to shut off my cell phone or turn off the radio in the car so I can make sure that my head is on straight when I get to the next meeting?" Be alert and aware of those things around you that might affect your mental acuity through the day and think about how to compensate for them.

Emotionally. "Where am I right now emotionally? Am I connected or detached? What am I feeling? What kind of mood am I in? What do I need to watch out for emotionally today? How can I control my response to stimuli so that my emotions do not take over?" Emotional acuity is our ability to feel deeply. This is normal and good, but the key is not to get stuck. We get angry but get over it quickly. We experience frustration but deal with it and move on. The question is how quickly and easily we can adapt emotionally to the challenges and changing circumstances of the day.

Spiritually. "Where am I right now spiritually? Why am I alive? Why am I on the planet? What is my purpose, and am I aligned with that purpose today?" Spiritual acuity is very important, because each day is too precious to waste and once gone will never come back. Being aligned spiritually does not just mean how religious we are. That may play a part, but essentially, spiritual alignment means being connected to our life purpose, whatever that may be for each of us. Do you know why you are here? What is your life purpose, and how well do you connect with it on a regular basis?

Physically. "Where am I right now physically? How do I feel? What are my energy levels and what must I do to master them today? What do I need to do physically today to equip myself to be focused and aligned? Am I eating correctly? Am I hydrating correctly? Am I getting enough movement and exercise through the day?" Be conscious of proper nutrition and of drinking enough water. Make sure to allow for some physical activity through the day, and don't forget periodic recovery breaks every 90 minutes.

One immediate benefit of this daily inventory is that it helps us identify our weakest link. Whichever of the four zones is weakest for us at any given time is the one that will "hemorrhage" under pressure. The weakest spot is where the leak will occur. Once we are aware of our weakest link, we can take steps to strengthen it.

My weakest link is physical. Because I fly all over the country, I fight jet lag on a regular basis. Because of my frequent travel, I eat out a lot and have learned to drink bottled water. Every city has different chemical additives in its water, which affect different people differently. Many travelers get sick while away and never even realize it is the water. There are so many things physically that I have to fight when traveling on a regular schedule that make physical acuity my weakest link, my most likely point of hemorrhage under pressure.

If I start to become distracted, I know it is not because I am "losing it" mentally, but that I am tired and need to get some physical recovery. I have learned by experience that when I am tired I get distracted easily. Emotionally, I may become short. Spiritually, I may be a little foggy about my purpose or sometimes even feel like quitting. I have learned, when these things happen, to look first to my physical acuity to see what may need attention there.

Where do you stand in your ability to navigate life successfully in each zone: mental, emotional, spiritual, and physical? Take a few minutes to complete the survey below. Be honest with yourself. This personal inventory will help you identify where you are in each area so you can better see where you need to go. It will also help you recognize your strengths and weaknesses, especially your "weakest link" so you can plan ahead to minimize "hemorrhaging" at that point.

SURVEY SYSTEM

Answer each question as it applies to your recent daily life at home and at work.

	1 poor–5 excellent				
Mental Zone					
How is your ability to focus under pressure?	**1**	**2**	**3**	**4**	**5**
How well can you concentrate under pressure?	**1**	**2**	**3**	**4**	**5**
How well do you navigate distractions throughout the day?	**1**	**2**	**3**	**4**	**5**
How well do you navigate confusion and indecision?	**1**	**2**	**3**	**4**	**5**
Emotional Zone					
How well do you navigate periods of moodiness?	**1**	**2**	**3**	**4**	**5**
How well do you navigate periods of being short-tempered?	**1**	**2**	**3**	**4**	**5**
How well do you trust others?	**1**	**2**	**3**	**4**	**5**
How well do you navigate life-change?	**1**	**2**	**3**	**4**	**5**
Spiritual Zone					
What is your level of personal fulfillment?	**1**	**2**	**3**	**4**	**5**
What is your level of professional fulfillment?	**1**	**2**	**3**	**4**	**5**
How satisfied are you with your life-purpose contribution?	**1**	**2**	**3**	**4**	**5**
How connected are you to what's most important to you?	**1**	**2**	**3**	**4**	**5**
Physical Zone					
How is your energy quality from morning to evening?	**1**	**2**	**3**	**4**	**5**
What is your ability to eat every three hours throughout the day?	**1**	**2**	**3**	**4**	**5**
How is your physical conditioning?	**1**	**2**	**3**	**4**	**5**
What is the frequency and effectiveness of your daily rest breaks?	**1**	**2**	**3**	**4**	**5**

Add all questions together for a total score.

75 – 80	Elite
65 – 75	Pro
55 – 65	Amateur
Below 55	Burn Out Zone

Daily alignment of our mind/body capacities is the most critical first step in successfully navigating our "aircraft" through the storm. Another part of the process is gaining a thorough understanding of each acuity and how it works, how it relates to the others, and how to care for and nurture it so it can be sharpened to its fullest. It is now time to look at each "system" of our aircraft in detail.

Chapter Three

Mission Critical Data

You need to play with supreme confidence,
or else you'll lose again, and then losing becomes a habit.

—Joe Paterno

ONE HOT SUMMER DAY SEVERAL years ago, I was playing baseball in the backyard with my son Brent, who was nine years old at the time. Brent is two years younger than Brandon. It was a friendly game of two-man whiffle ball, where if the batter hit the ball and the other player hit him with the ball while he was running the bases, the batter was out. I was at bat and Brent was pitching and fielding.

I hit one pitch that sent the ball way over toward the house. Brent went dashing after it as I started rounding the bases. He was running full speed, looking back and forth between me and the ball to gauge when and where to throw it so he could hit me. Brent was always hyperactive, like a buzz saw, and was so intent on snagging that ball that he did not watch where he was going. He was running full-out on a collision course with a double glass sliding door. With a growing sense of horror I could see what was coming. It was almost like slow motion. I yelled out to Brent, but he was so focused on the ball that he did not hear me. At the last moment, he realized what was happening and put his arms up, but it was too late. Brent plowed right through that glass door without even slowing down. That was when we discovered that the door did not have safety glass. Shattered glass flew everywhere.

Sandy was sitting on the couch watching television and eating ice cream. As soon as Brent hit that door, Sandy threw her bowl in the air. Ice cream was all over the living room. I jumped through the shattered door right behind Brent in time to see him standing in the living room while Sandy carefully removed a large shard of glass that was embedded in his forearm. She was afraid that all his moving around would cause him to rip himself up more. Like a knife, that fragment of glass filleted Brent's arm to the bone from his wrist to his elbow; it just laid it wide open.

By this time, Sandy was almost hysterical. Brandon was in the other room watching television. Brent was screaming and starting to go into shock, so I picked him up and carried him through the house to the front yard where we could sit and wait for the ambulance to arrive. Both of us were covered with blood. I took a closer look at Brent's arm. Muscles, tendons, and raw flesh were in full view. As Brent saw the damage he said, "Dad, I'm going to die! I'm going to die!"

"No, you won't," I reassured him. "God will take care of you." Brent was starting to turn pale from pre-shock, so to get his mind off the injury itself I asked, "Have you ever seen muscles and tendons at work?"

"No, Dad," Brent replied softly, "have you?"

I made a comment about how wonderfully God had made us and that this was a perfect opportunity to study His handiwork. I said, "Look at your arm." He did. "Now, move your fingers." He wiggled his fingers and we could see the muscles in his arm move. By now, Brent's arm was numb from the natural morphine his body had secreted, so he couldn't really feel anything. Brent said, "Wow, that's pretty interesting."

By taking Brent's focus off his injury and onto the wonder of anatomy, I helped delay his going into shock. I covered his arm back up, hugged him, and we sat and talked until the ambulance arrived. Inside, the house was mass confusion as Sandy spoke with the 911 operator and the television was blaring so that the sound of the ambulance arriving would not provoke an untimely seizure in Brandon.

At the hospital, Brent underwent five hours of surgery, including plastic surgery, and came through just fine. The amazing thing is that the shard of glass came out at exactly the same angle that it went in, so that it did not cut any muscles, tendons, veins, or arteries. Today, a scar is the only evidence of Brent's ordeal. He suffered no paralysis or permanent damage. It is truly a miracle.

Chaos is a weird thing. It affects people differently at different times. In this particular crisis, Sandy freaked out but I clicked into work mode. I was calm, I picked Brent up and carried him outside so he wouldn't bleed on the carpet, sat down with him, talked gently with him, went to the hospital with him, talked with the surgeons, and sat with him while they did the blood test and put him to sleep for surgery. Later, around 9:00 p.m., I was alone in the waiting room. Everyone else was gone, Sandy had returned home to be with Brandon, and the pressure was off. I had done everything I could, and matters were now out of my hands. *That's* when *I* fell apart.

When the crisis came, my training kicked in. Training equips us to deal with the hard times so that we can do what needs to be done when it needs to be done. That is why we will never consistently outperform our training. Hard times will trigger our training, but to be effective against hard times, that training must include conditioning in *life toughness.*

Life Toughness

If we compare navigating life's storms to flying an airplane, the first thing we need is our "flight plan." This is our *mission critical data*, the information that is absolutely critical for us to know in order to navigate successfully. Because it involves knowledge, *mission critical data* relates to the *mental* zone of our being.

Research and training have identified six markers that help define the parameters of our *mission critical data*. The first three markers relate to the factor of *life toughness*. What makes someone tough? How do we get tough in life? Usually, what toughens us are the things that go wrong, the things that beat up on us, the hard knocks that we learn from. Young children learn not to touch fire by getting burned. They learn not to fall against the end of a table when they bust an eye open. All of us spend time studying in the school of hard knocks. Experience truly is the best teacher.

Training can help shorten the gap, but even training carries bumps of its own. One purpose of training is to educate and develop people in *life toughness*, which is defined by three specific markers, or characteristic elements. The first of these is to be *strong*. Tough individuals are strong *mentally*, *emotionally*, *spiritually*, and *physically*. They have a depth or reservoir of strength that when you knock them down, they don't stay down. They're just tough. I played football in high school and learned very quickly who the tough guys were: the ones you could hit and hit and hit and keep on hitting, and they would just stand there.

Strength is important because if we are not strong enough in any of these zones, we will be dominated by an opponent who is stronger. If we allow other people to get in our heads, they will dominate us, and if we are not tough, it will hurt us. Suddenly, we feel as though we have to defend ourselves, to attack those who have attacked us. That is not so. If we are strong enough to know who we are, it does not matter what anybody else says.

Most often we think of strength as being something physical, but toughness in life involves being strong in the other three zones as well: *mentally* capable of logical and rational thinking, *emotionally* grounded and stable, and *spiritually* connected firmly to one's life purpose.

The second marker for *life toughness* is to be *flexible*. Strength without flexibility will lead eventually to injury. Without flexibility, even the strongest athletes in the world would get hurt sooner or later. Strength alone is not enough; it must be joined with flexibility because flexibility helps protect against injury. Athletes do plenty of strength training, but they also work diligently on flexibility and agility. They are always stretching and pulling so that when the strain and pressure come they can bend without breaking.

Those who are not strong enough will be dominated and those who are strong enough but not flexible will get hurt. Every day countless people get hurt *mentally*, *emotionally*, *spiritually*, or *physically*. They are *mentally* distracted and *emotionally* erratic and don't know why. *Spiritually*, they have lost sight of their purpose and *physically*, they are always fighting against low energy levels. No matter how strong we are, we need flexibility so that when life throws a monkey wrench into our plans, we can adapt.

The third ingredient to life toughness is to be *resilient.* Whoever is not strong enough will be dominated, whoever is not flexible enough will get hurt, and whoever is not resilient enough will eventually quit. I know plenty of people who simply gave up. They stopped five feet from the goal, thinking they were still ten miles away. They quit because they felt they simply had nothing more to give.

Resilience is important because it enables us to keep coming back for more. Success does not mean that we never get knocked down. Success means that we get up *one more time* than we are knocked down. Defeat is not failure. Failure is when we let defeat become *final.*

Navigating Life Storms

The second major factor of our *mission critical data* is *navigating life storms.* Here, as with life toughness, there are three markers that define and identify the degrees or levels at which we may navigate life: *survive, function,* or *thrive.* It's hard enough to fly a plane even on a good day. Sometimes life can be tough even when things are going well. Storms add seasoning to the mixture by revealing our true character and how prepared or unprepared we are for the crisis. Training helps determine the level at which we navigate—whether we *survive, function,* or *thrive*—as well as how quickly we transition from lower to higher levels.

At the low end of life navigation is the level of seeking simply to *survive.* Survival mode is a kind of "automatic pilot." Run by the autonomic nervous system and hardwired into our low brain, survival mode is an unconscious response mechanism to recognize and respond to threat or danger. The autonomic nervous system controls all the automatic, involuntary processes of our body, such as heartbeat, respiration, body temperature, circulation, oxygen levels, blood/oxygen mixture, blinking, etc.

Survival mode is a "fight or flight" response that focuses our attention on what we *absolutely must do right now* in order to stay alive. At 9:00 a.m. on September 11, 2001 in south Manhattan, no one in the World Trade Center was worried about the stock market or the economy. No one was thinking about his 401(k) or her upcoming vacation. At that moment, those people were focused on one thing: *getting out of those buildings*. In survival mode, we *act* first, *then* think. It is a reflex. We don't have to actually touch the fire before an autonomic response jerks our hand away from the flame. When life's storms hit, our instinct for survival kicks in.

There is nothing wrong with survival mode; it is a natural first step in navigating through a storm. A storm disrupts the normal flow of life and puts everything in a state of flux. In the ensuing chaos, everyone goes into survival mode until they can assess the situation, see what needs to be done, and make adjustments. Survival is also the first priority for virtually any new endeavor–a new business, a new marriage, a new job, a new house. Undertaking a new challenge usually involves a learning curve, and the tricky part is keeping everything else going while the learning takes place.

Unfortunately, some people get stuck in survival mode and stay there for so long that they no longer know anything different. These are the individuals who end up with anxiety disorders, panic attacks, depression, mood swings, and all sorts of distractibility issues.

Every human entity, whether an individual, family, or institution, passes through an initial survival phase. Some do not make it, but most do. Survival mode is supposed to be a temporary state, the first "port in the storm," so to speak. At some point, however, survival mode should give way to *function* mode.

Function mode is where most people live on a day-to-day basis, at least in the United States. Even though the majority of them thrive from time to time, few ever rise to the level where they thrive consistently. The figures are not exact, but probably around 20 percent of people in America merely *survive*, while perhaps 70 percent *function*. Only 10 percent of the population *thrive* consistently, if that many.

People at the *function* level often are very content with their lives. After all, people who function handle the daily challenges of life with a fair degree of balance. They hold an even keel, they get the job done, they earn a living, they support their families, they raise their children, they get involved in their communities. Life is good.

The primary drawback to the *function* mode is that it is essentially a *maintenance* level. People expend so much time, energy, and effort *functioning* that they have little left to help them rise higher. The *function* mode is average or above average performance, and people who live at that level rarely tap into their full potential. Those who *do*, however, and who learn to do so consistently, enter the rarefied atmosphere of the few who *thrive*.

Most of the time, the reason people fail to thrive is because they have not been trained how. They don't know what to do, what to look for, how to evaluate where they are, or how to chart where they want to go. Training can make all the difference. Through training, a person who is only functioning now can learn how to thrive as a way of life, and perform at their peak *under pressure, on demand.*

The *thrive* level represents the upper echelon of achievement and performance excellence. People who *thrive* deliver excellence not occasionally, or even frequently, but *consistently*. In every area of life—professional, personal, and family—they have learned how to align their *mental*, *emotional*, *spiritual*, and *physical* zones, and are steadily releasing more and more of their potential. Ninety-five percent of people work for someone else; only five percent work for themselves. There are fewer people at the top because it is harder to reach. The evolution from *surviving* to *functioning* to *thriving* is a compression ratio—the higher we rise, the tougher it gets.

Many high school athletes dream of playing professionally, but only a tiny fraction of them realize that dream. First comes college, where the qualifying bar for varsity sports is higher than in high school. This is where a significant number wash out. Those who make the grade into college athletics face even more daunting competition in their pursuit of the pros. Less than one percent of all college athletes ever make it into the professional leagues.

It's like gravity. We can't beat gravity, so we must learn how to work with it. The Wright brothers succeeded in building the first powered airplane because they stopped trying to overcome the force of gravity and learned how to make gravity work *for* them. Once they learned how to navigate the realities of the situation, they learned how to fly. Life is the same way. Most people dream of flying, but some never really get off the ground. They *survive*, but that's it. Many more make it into the air regularly (*function*), but only a very few ever soar (*thrive*). For most people, the problem lies not in a lack of talent or ability, but in a lack of training. The average person is not trained to fly.

EVOLUTIONS AND TRANSITIONS

One of the reasons many of us so often have trouble dealing with storms in life is because mentally we are locked into looking at time in only one way, as an ongoing sequence of seconds, minutes, hours, and days. Modern western society is bound by the clock. We "punch in" at the beginning of the workday and "punch out" at the end. Our daily schedules are regulated by where we have to be at any given hour. We divide our days into precise units of time. Within reason, this is not necessarily a bad thing because it helps us plan and organize for greater productivity and better performance. If, for example, we want to attend a seminar across the country, we need to be time-conscious enough to make sure we are at the airport in time for our flight's scheduled departure.

There is another way to look at the relationship between life and time. As much as it may be measured by a sequence of precise units of time, life is also a continuing progression of *evolutions* and *transitions*. Evolution is a process of change in a certain direction. Transitions are the necessary periods of adjustment between evolutions. Evolutions are life as it happens; transitions are the storms. In the analogy of flying, a storm is the transition between two areas of calm air. A life storm is the transition that carries us from one reality (evolution) to another changed or adjusted reality.

Military units, and Special Forces in particular, are trained to think in terms of evolutions. Navy SEALs don't watch the clock, punching in at 9:00 and punching out at 5:00. When they are operating in the field, they are on evolutions. Their current mission is their evolution, and they will stay until it is completed. Whether the evolution is three days or three weeks, they stay focused on completing their mission. They could lie down in the woods for three days camouflaged by leaves, rarely moving, and no one would ever know they were there. The reason they can do it is because in their heads it's an evolution. They don't think in terms of completing a "three-day mission," but of finishing the evolution. This requires a whole new mind-set, a completely different way of thinking from normal society.

All of us pass through evolutions in our lives *mentally*, *emotionally*, *spiritually*, and *physically*. For example, going to school is a mental evolution. We study and cram and take tests and fill our heads with a lot of knowledge that at the time we cannot imagine that we will ever use. Eventually we graduate, however, get a job, and start applying what we learned. That is a second evolution. The first evolution was data storage; the second is application of stored data. We live our lives in evolutions that ebb and flow, but that ebb and flow is different for each person.

A transition is the segue between two evolutions. Anyone who has ever struggled with theme writing in English class knows that transitional sentences and paragraphs are the hardest of all to write. Their purpose is to link sections of the text together so that they mesh into a logical flow. Often, more time is spent writing transitional sentences than in writing the body of the theme itself.

In the same way, transitions are the hardest times in our lives because they whip us out of one evolution and sling us into another one. Transitions give us a dose of clear-eyed reality, and they are not always friendly. Going from middle school to high school is a stark reality check. So is going from high school to college. Making the change from college to the work world is a stark reality check. Getting married is a *big* reality check. Having a child is another one.

Evolutions in life tend to get tougher as we go, but the transitions often are even more difficult. At the same time, transitions usually contain the greatest opportunities for learning, because if we can figure out the current transition, we can predict the next evolution with a pretty high degree of accuracy. Once we learn both to view transitions as a positive process for moving us from point A to point B, and to predict the next evolution, we can start living in greater control of our lives, instead of being out of control.

Dealing With Personal Storms

It's time for an exercise. At this point during live training sessions I always ask the group two questions and allow several minutes for them to jot down their answers. The questions are designed to help them assess their understanding of *mission critical data* by bringing it out of the realm of theory and making it personal, and to help them be open and honest about their own individual circumstances. Now it's your turn. Think carefully about these questions. Take some time to write down your thoughts and ideas. Be honest with yourself. Periodic honest self-evaluation is healthy and beneficial.

What kind of storms have you endured in the past year? Remember, a storm can be anything that disrupts any area of life: personal, professional, relational, mental, emotional, spiritual, or physical. Maybe you moved. Maybe you got a job, changed jobs, or lost a job. Perhaps you got married. Perhaps you got divorced. Perhaps you had a baby. You may have lost a parent, a spouse, or a child. You may have started college, or finished college. Perhaps you or someone close to you was diagnosed with cancer or some other serious illness. What has happened in the past year to interrupt or impede the smooth flow of life? What challenges have you faced? Identifying and acknowledging your personal storms is the first step to dealing with them.

How have you adapted to your storms? How well did you weather the storm? What condition were you in when you reached the other side? Did you adapt in a healthy manner?

Did you find yourself to be *strong, flexible,* and *resilient,* or did the storm overpower you? As a result of the storm, where are you now? Are you *thriving,* are you *functioning,* or are you merely *surviving*? How do you know if you have adapted well? Someone might say, "I gained ten pounds." That is not healthy adaptation. "I lose sleep," or "I'm sleepy all the time," or "I'm depressed"; these are signs of poor adaptation. "I have trouble focusing," or "I don't like being around people anymore," or "I don't exercise as much," or "I eat too much," or "I eat too little"; all of these indicate trouble with adapting to storms.

We all have certain behaviors and tendencies that we are inclined to fall back on when going through a storm. The way we respond to, or transition through, a storm tends to be the same time after time, and reveals how well we have learned to adapt. Some people spend money, especially money they don't have. Others get drunk, or do drugs, or act crazy or hang out with the wrong people. This is called *compensatory behavior*—overcompensating in one area to make up for the feeling that something is wrong in another area. They go overboard seeking pleasure in an effort to escape the pain and discomfort of the storm.

How we transition in a storm depends on whether we resort to compensatory behavior or respond with *preferred behavior*—deliberate, positive actions we take that are designed to get us through the storm successfully. The key is, first, to identify our personal weakest link, the place where we slip most easily into compensatory behavior and, second, to train ourselves to do the opposite. For example, if your weakest link happens to be physical, as mine is, you may discover that when a storm comes, you let yourself go. You stop eating right and drinking right, you stop exercising; in general you become lazy and lethargic physically. If you know *beforehand* that this is the way you tend to react in a storm, you can make deliberate plans to change your behavior the next time. Instead of letting your body go during a storm, you can train yourself to make sure you continue to eat properly, hydrate properly, exercise regularly, and get sufficient sleep.

When a baseball player goes into a batting slump and has trouble hitting the ball, the batting coach will take him back to the batter's box and review the basics. How are you standing? Are you dropping your shoulder? Are you keeping your eyes on the ball? It is the same in any other sport. A golfer who is off on his game will work with a pro who will take him back to the fundamentals. You're turning your hand when you swing. You have too strong a grip.

When we struggle making the transition through a storm, going back to basics is the quickest way to fix it. Many times our difficulty lies with the fact that we focus on the wrong things, things that have nothing to do with the problem. Don't forget the 90/10 rule. As long as we concentrate our efforts on the 10 percent of reality that we cannot change, we will continue to be frustrated. What good will it do to curse the weather because of the storm? What will we accomplish by wishing that people would "act right"? When will *that* happen? It hasn't happened in 6,000 years of human history, and it's not going to change now. We need to fix our attention on the 90 percent of reality that we can change. Most of the time we cannot change the circumstances that bring about a storm, but we can change how we respond to the storm.

Jump With Purpose

Successful advance planning for positive response in storms calls for making specific, well thought-out decisions. We all make hundreds of decisions every day, both large and small: what to eat, what to wear, what work task to tackle first, whether or not to obey the speed limit, which stocks to buy and which ones to sell, which car to purchase, what groceries to buy, etc. Because of the way our minds are wired, every decision we make is irreversible. You may say, "I changed my mind." No, you didn't; you simply made a new decision based on an earlier decision. Another inaccurate statement is to say, "I can't decide." You already *did*. Not to decide is a *decision* not to decide. Not to decide is a *decision* to postpone *another* decision.

Our English word "decide" is derived from the Latin word *decidere*, which literally means "to cut off" or to eliminate. "Suicide" and "homicide" have their root in the same Latin word. In a similar way, the words "decision," "incision," and "excision" are related. To decide, then, literally means to eliminate every other choice or option. One image I use regularly in training is of a man jumping from an airplane and floating to earth in a parachute. At that moment, can he "change his mind" and return to the aircraft? No. Now that he has jumped, he is committed. When he "*decidered*" from that plane, he eliminated the choice to stay aboard. For the next several minutes he will be occupied in making many small decisions based on the big decision he made to step out of that airplane: when to pull the ripcord, where to land, how to stay out of the trees or the water, etc.

Understanding how we make decisions is vital in learning how to navigate life's storms. We need to be careful to put enough time, thought, and energy into our decisions, especially the big ones, so that we can make the right choices. I hate going into grocery stores unprepared. It's like stimuli overload. They don't have just cereal; they have a whole *row* of cereal. They don't have just soup; they have an entire *shelf* of soup. I try to make my decisions *before* I go to the grocery store; that way, I already know what I'm after.

I'm no different from anybody else. Most of us make a grocery list before we go to the store. Where we run into trouble is when we deviate from our list. That's when we start buying "comfort" food rather than nutritional food. We're depressed, so we buy Twinkies® because they make us feel good. There is a distinct psychology behind the layout of a grocery store. Related items are stocked close together, as if to suggest, "If you are buying *that*, then you probably need *this* also, to go with it." Do you think it is an accident that "impulse" items are stocked on shelves at the checkout lines? If we don't go in with a plan, and stick to that plan, our whole "mission" can become skewed.

Like a parachutist who makes sure everything is in order and understands his objective before ever leaving the airplane, we also need to learn to "jump with purpose" in our decision making. As simple as this may sound, it can be very difficult to practice. This is true in the corporate world as much as it is in private life. Many companies trap themselves by making major decisions based upon skewed data, only to discover years or millions of dollars down the line that those decisions ran at cross-purposes to the company's mission statement and bottom line.

The most successful companies are those that understand their purpose and their market, and make all their corporate decisions accordingly. Here is a case in point. For a decade and a half, Walgreens® outperformed its nearest competitor by a billion dollars in profit because it stayed true to a protocol of how it was going to buy new stores, where those stores would be located, and how they would operate. While the competitor was committed to growth, it adopted a strategy of expanding and venturing out into many different areas. In addition to being a pharmacy, the competitor wanted to be a grocery store, a "feel good" type of store, a store that would be "all things to all people."

Walgreens® took a different approach. The company said, "We want to be the most *convenient* drug store on the planet." Consequently, they always tried to purchase a corner lot so that their customers would have fast, easy access from two or three directions. This was such a fundamental part of their strategy that the company would spend a million dollars to move an existing store down the street just to occupy a corner lot that they did not previously have. They regarded this as an investment because they knew it would eventually return to them in profit.

Everything was geared to the convenience of the customer. Walgreens® was committed to a customer-friendly environment in location, product line, sales, and service. They were the innovators in drive-up pharmacy, because they wanted to be convenient for their customers. While the competitor focused on profitability and building more stores, Walgreens® focused on the customer.

In one area of San Francisco, California, there are *nine* Walgreens® stores within a one-mile radius. Why? San Francisco is laid out in grids with large blocks. Walgreens® did not want their customers to have to walk very far, so they put up a store on one side of the street, and another on the other side of the street, and another around the corner, and so forth. On the surface, it might appear to be a strange and self-defeating strategy to put so many stores of the same chain so close together, yet they blew the competition away.

Walgreens® succeeded because they "jumped with purpose." They knew who they were and what they were after *before* they started, and that understanding influenced and guided their corporate decisions. Impulsive decisions often lead to trouble. Many people live reckless, haphazard, unfulfilled, mediocre, and even tragic lives simply because they make impulsive decisions. The unhealthiest decisions we make are the ones we don't think through. Instead of jumping with purpose, we shoot from the hip. Before long, we wake up and ask, "How in the world did I get here?" That's why our ability to make sound decisions is so important. Success is never final and rarely is it accidental. Consistent success comes with discipline, determination, planning, training, and sound decision-making.

Bunny in the Box

Making sound decisions requires access to reliable and accurate information. Depending on what is at stake, poor information could lead to faulty decisions with potentially disastrous results. In closely timed and coordinated military operations, there is always the danger of "friendly fire," where combat units, ships, or aircraft, often relying on erroneous information, accidentally attack their own troops. This is why one of the fundamental principles of combat training is to verify one's target before firing.

Military pilots call target verification training the "bunny in the box." Modern fighter jets are equipped with a "heads-up display," where aircraft status, navigational information, weapons status, targeting information, and other such *mission critical data* are projected visually onto the windshield of the cockpit. In this way, the pilot can fly and stay constantly abreast of the condition and status of his aircraft without having to move his head.

Part of the heads-up display is the targeting display, a rectangular box with a crosshair in the center. The "bunny" is the target, and the object is to get the "bunny" into the box and under the crosshairs before pulling the trigger. Unless the "bunny" is in the box, the aircraft's weapons are not aligned properly with the target, and to fire at that point could result in high collateral damage. Pilots spend many hours in flight simulators training to get the "bunny in the box" so that when they get into a real combat situation they will be able to hit their designated targets consistently.

Decision-making is like that. We need to be sure we know what we are aiming at before we fire. Too often in our lives we shoot from the hip like a fighter jet that is indiscriminately dropping bombs or firing missiles, and then wonder why there is so much debris around us. We are quick to fire but slow to consider the collateral damage or logical fallout that may result from our actions or hasty or ill-considered decisions.

Each of us must bear responsibility for what we do. We can't say, "I'm sorry, but I was so busy and running so fast. I'm doing the best I can." Making excuses won't cut it. Fighter pilots who keep missing targets won't be fighter pilots very long. Before we pull the trigger or make a decision, whether at work, at home, or elsewhere, we need to make sure that the "bunny is in the box"—that the decision is aligned in the crosshairs of what we want our lives to be. Otherwise, we will inflict heavy collateral damage on our lives and the lives of those around us.

Every fighter jet has a computer system designed to assist the pilot in getting the bunny in the box. As the pilot approaches the target area, he flips open the cover over the trigger button, which activates the weapons system. At that point he hears a steady beeping sound in the headset of his helmet, a warning beep that says, "Your weapons are hot; keep your finger off the trigger until you are sure of your target." Once the target is lined up in the crosshairs—once the bunny is in the box—the steady beeping changes to one sustained beep, which means, "You are locked on the target; fire when ready." The computer will do the rest.

That's alignment, and that's what we're after. Before we make decisions in life, particularly major or semi-major decisions, we need to make sure that we align that bunny in the box and hear that tone before we pull that trigger. Are we prepared for the consequences of our actions? Can we live with the results of our decision?

In summary, *mission critical data* is the mental acuity part of life navigation, that information which is absolutely vital for us to know in order to navigate storms successfully. It involves three things, essentially. First is the understanding of life toughness issues, of knowing that we have the strength, flexibility, and resilience to face the storm. Second is knowing what to do when the storm hits so that we can transition as quickly as possible from survival mode, adapting through the storm so that we can learn to thrive in spite of it. Third is the knowledge that we are personally responsible for the actions we take and the decisions we make, and therefore must give great thought and care to them beforehand. When these three areas are properly aligned, we are equipped *mentally* for peak performance *under pressure, on demand.*

Prevailing Under Pressure

Many people may remember retired Admiral Jim Stockdale as H. Ross Perot's vice-presidential running mate in the 1992 presidential election. There is much more to the admiral's story, however, than just his brief foray into politics. His eight-year ordeal as a prisoner of the North Vietnamese is a clear illustration of how positive mental acuity and alignment help provide the strength, flexibility, and resilience necessary not only to survive a life storm, but to thrive in spite of it and triumph over it. His is a story of prevailing under pressure.

At the height of the Vietnam conflict, Admiral Stockdale was the highest-ranking American military officer in the "Hanoi Hilton" prisoner-of-war camp. From 1965 to 1973 he endured repeated tortures, privation, and severe hardship, with no idea of when he would be released or if he would see his family again. As the ranking officer, he also took on the burden of responsibility for the welfare of the other prisoners. Finally released in 1973, Stockdale was a national hero and Congressional Medal of Honor winner and went on to become a student of philosophy and a successful author.

Years later, when asked how he survived his imprisonment without breaking, Stockdale replied,

> I never lost faith in the end of the story...I never doubted not only that I would get out, but also that I would prevail in the end and turn the experience into the defining event of my life, which, in retrospect, I would not trade.[1]

He went on to say that the prisoners who didn't make it were the optimists who continually held out that they would be free by a particular date: Christmas, Easter, Thanksgiving, etc. When time after time it didn't happen, they gradually lost hope and died. Admiral Stockdale, while never doubting that he would one day be free, refused to assign a specific time frame for his release. Although he firmly believed he would eventually prevail, at the same time he fully acknowledged the grim circumstances of his current reality. This seemingly contradictory mix of blind faith and rugged realism came to be

1. Jim Collins, *Good to Great: Why Some Companies Make the Leap...and Others Don't* (New York: HarperCollins Publishers, 2001), 84.

known as the "Stockdale paradox." The admiral himself stated it this way:

> You must never confuse faith that you will prevail in the end—which you can never afford to lose—with the discipline to confront the most brutal facts of your current reality, whatever they might be.[2]

Admiral Stockdale prevailed over the life storm of his imprisonment and torture in large part because his mental and spiritual acuities were aligned and gave him the strength, flexibility, and resilience to weather the storm. Mentally, he accepted the harsh reality of his current circumstances, and spiritually he never lost faith that he would win, never lost sight of who he was, and never forgot all the reasons he had for living. Beyond simply surviving his ordeal, Stockdale thrived as a result. His experience in the "Hanoi Hilton" and how he survived propelled him to greater excellence later, and became, in his words, the "defining event" of his life.

That's what life toughness is all about: standing strong, flexible, and resilient in the gale, transforming the storm from a potentially destructive force into a catalyst that propels us to excellence.

---

2. Jim Collins, *Good to Great: Why Some Companies Make the Leap...and Others Don't* (New York: HarperCollins Publishers, 2001), 85.

Chapter Four

Instrument Navigation

Do what you can, with what you have, where you are.

—Theodore Roosevelt

Every pilot needs a flight plan, the *mission critical data* that tells him where to go and how to get there. In life this means that our mental acuity needs to be honed to a fine edge so that we can operate from an informed *situational awareness* with the *strength*, *flexibility*, and *resilience* necessary to navigate the storms that come our way.

Beyond the flight plan, pilots also must understand their instruments, the dials, gauges, and other indicators that continually display condition and status of the aircraft and its systems. Military and commercial pilots must be instrument-rated, meaning they must be capable of flying "blind," operating on instruments alone.

Instrument navigation in flight equates to emotional navigation in life. Performance *under pressure, on demand* requires a clear understanding of our emotional makeup as well as the connection that exists between our emotions, our energy levels, and our speed of recovery. Our emotions are the instrument gauges of our life. Neither good nor bad, they simply respond to stimuli. Emotions gauge the various stimuli that are imported through our five physiological senses of sight, smell, taste, touch, and hearing, and our sixth sense of spiritual perception. Whatever stimulates our senses triggers emotional responses. Our biggest challenge is learning to interpret those responses and what they mean to us.

Because emotions can be so complicated and confusing, many of us quite often try to handle them by dealing only with the emotions themselves without addressing the conditions or circumstances that triggered them. Imagine that you're driving down the highway when the oil pressure warning indicator lights up on your car's instrument panel. You're too busy to stop, flying as you are down the road of life at Mach 2 with your hair on fire, so you reach under the dashboard and pop the bulb out. The warning light goes off. Problem solved—or so you think. Ten miles down the road your engine seizes up and you come to a grinding, wrenching halt.

In life, as with cars, that's the danger we face when we treat the symptoms instead of the cause. The problem does not go away; it merely bides its time under the surface for awhile until it manifests itself in greater force later. When it comes to our emotions, we often tend to work the symptoms rather than solve the problem. If we do not know how to read our emotions and have little idea how our emotions affect our physiology, we will be ill equipped to deal with the emotional storms of life. We must make sure that, instead of treating only the symptoms, we learn to use our emotional "tracking system" to help us understand what is going on "under the hood," so to speak. *Emotional* acuity, our *instrument navigation,* is critical to our ability to weather life's storms.

Emotions and Performance

Feelings influence performance but are not criteria for it. We can perform—do what we need to do—even when we do not feel like it. I played football in high school, and during the summer it was common for us to practice twice a day, once in the morning and once in the afternoon. During the two-hour break in between I usually went home to eat lunch and rest.

Throughout high school I had periodic problems with one of my knees. Even after surgery it would occasionally swell up painfully. One day I came dragging in after the afternoon practice. It was hot, my knee was swollen, I was limping, and I felt absolutely whipped. As I walked in, my mother said, "Terry, it's your week to mow the lawn, and you need to do it today."

I remember saying, "Mom, I don't feel like mowing the lawn today. Could it wait until tomorrow?"

She looked at me, and replied, "Son, if feelings were criteria for doing something, you would be dead. When you were a baby, I didn't always feel like waking up in the middle of the night to feed you, but I did it anyway. I didn't always feel like stopping whatever I was doing just to change your diaper, but I did it anyway. When you were a toddler and tried to run in the street chasing balls, I didn't always feel like running after you to keep you from getting hit by a car, but I did it anyway."

Needless to say, I mowed the lawn that day, and learned a valuable lesson at the same time: *Feelings are not a criteria for performance*. Some days you just have to suck it up and do what you have to do.

Nevertheless, a relationship does exist between performance and emotion. Our emotional state affects our speed of recovery, which, in turn, affects our performance. This is because our emotions and our energy levels are interconnected. Emotion and energy go together. They are inseparable, like the components of gasoline.

Gasoline consists of two parts, a liquid base and a fume or octane base, which gives the gasoline its explosiveness. Whenever we pull into a gas station to refuel our car, we have a choice between several octane levels. The higher the octane, the hotter the fuel burns, and the hotter it burns, the purer it burns. Higher octane gasoline ignites faster and burns cleaner and more efficiently than does lower octane. The high performance engines of professional race cars require fuel with an octane level 20-30 percent higher than anything available on the street. Gasoline that hot would burn up ordinary engines.

It is the same way with emotions and energy. At any given moment we operate from either a high or low energy level–a positive or a negative–with a corresponding emotional state. For example, excitement and high energy go together; so do exhaustion and low energy. A person in a high emotion/energy state will have a bounce in their step and vigor in their movements. Their face and body language will mirror their high energy level. They are consuming high-octane fuel, burning and pumping on all cylinders. Likewise, someone who is tired will show it in their actions and demeanor, moping and dragging around at a very low octane energy level.

The word *emotion* is derived from a root meaning, "to move." *Emotion*, then, literally means "to set in motion." That motion will be either positive or negative, high or low. To be without emotion is to be dead. Life manifests itself in our bodies in numerous ways, and one of the most significant is through emotion. Like stress, emotions have gotten a bad rap in recent years. Emotions are the gauges that tell us that we are alive. The issue is not emotions, but learning how to navigate our emotional landscape. We do this first by identifying the energy level or emotional quadrant we are operating from (high or low, positive or negative) and then, if necessary, making the transition from where we are to where we want to be emotionally.

NAVIGRAM AWARENESS

Sometimes, in dealing with intangible things such as emotions, a graphic representation can aid in our understanding. The following chart or "navigram" will help us visualize where we are on the emotional landscape, as well as how our emotions relate to each other. I call this a "navigram" because it is an aid in navigating the often confusing terrain of our emotional zone.

Navigram Awareness

–	+
Angry Fearful Frustrated Anxious	Excited Connected Challenged Pumped
Sad Depressed Lonely Exhausted	Calm Peaceful Relaxed Recharged

– **Emotions** +

Through this navigram, we can classify our emotions as falling into one of four different quadrants, each of which has a particular energy level associated with it. The two quadrants on the right are positive, meaning they house positive emotions, while the two on the left contain negative emotions. At the upper right is the *high positive* quadrant, characterized by *positive* emotions with a *high* energy level. The emotional state of this quadrant can be described with words such as *excited, connected, challenged,* and *pumped.* Below this is the *low positive* quadrant of *positive* emotions with a *low* energy level. In this quadrant we feel *calm, peaceful, relaxed,* and *recharged.* It is where we recharge our batteries. To the left is the *low negative* quadrant of *low* energy *negative* emotions such as when we are *sad, depressed, lonely,* or *exhausted.* This is where we find ourselves when we are out of gas emotionally. Finally, at the upper left is the *high negative* quadrant of *high* energy *negative* emotions. We are in this quadrant when we feel *angry, fearful, frustrated,* or *anxious.*

These four emotional quadrants are separated by lines that represent a membrane or barrier that we must pass through when moving from one quadrant to another. Emotionally, we are always moving between quadrants. Sometimes something happens that drags us from one quadrant to another; at other times, we make a deliberate choice to move. Someone may make us angry, propelling us into the high negative quadrant, but we *choose* how long to stay angry. Circumstances may cause us to feel frustrated, but how long we *choose* to stay that way is up to us. At some point, *every* emotion—sadness, depression, excitement, calmness, joy—becomes a choice.

Clinical depression is different because it is chemically induced by the depletion of serotonin in the brain, and treatment with chemicals or an antidepressant may be needed. Acute depression, on the other hand, is caused usually by negative external circumstances—loss of a job, loss of a family member, financial reversal, etc.—and is normally temporary in nature. In most cases, these are things we can do something about. A positive change in circumstances or adjusting to the altered reality will take care of it. Acute depression can be described as focusing on the wrong thing for too long, until that thing becomes our reality.

The 90/10 rule says that 90 percent of reality is *perception*, and 10 percent is *unchanging*. Many people get stuck in a negative emotional quadrant for too long either because they don't know how to navigate out of it, or they spend 90 percent of their time trying to change the 10 percent of reality that will never change. Gravity will always be in force; the sun will always rise in the east; we will always have to pay taxes; we will always have to deal with people. These are unchanging realities.

One of the first keys to navigating our emotions is learning to identify what is changeable in our lives and what is not. If something is within our power to change, fine; if not, we have to learn to let it go. Understanding this difference gives us a lot of room to move around in emotionally. It is not what *happens* to us that defines us in life. What defines us in life is how we *respond* to what happens to us. Response is everything.

Another key to emotional navigation is recognizing that we must have some type of active or passive recovery to bring us back from the negative side to the positive side. It is much harder to be positive than negative; from ten to fifteen times harder, according to some studies. Staying positive emotionally takes work and deliberate effort. All we have to do to be negative is show up. Many times, we have to cross that membrane from negative to positive by direct and deliberate intent. We need some type of recovery mechanism for making that transition.

If we are angry, fearful, frustrated, exhausted, sad, depressed, etc., how can we move from the negative to the positive side quickly? Take a simple break. We talked about it earlier. Get a change of focus. Talk to somebody. Listen to music. Laugh. Get some exercise. Read a book. The possibilities are virtually endless. There are different kinds of recovery, and not every method works well with everyone. Each of us must find the ones that work best for us.

Emotions and Physical Health

Recovery and transition are important for both our emotional and physical health. Prolonged periods in the negative emotional quadrants make us susceptible to all sorts of health problems. This is particularly true of the high negative quadrant, which is the most toxic of all. Strong negative emotions such as anger, fear, or anxiety trigger in our bodies the release of a chemical called *cortisol.* Loaded through the central nervous system, *cortisol* is a "fight or flight" response chemical that helps us recognize and respond to danger.

Let's say that we are driving down the highway, and someone cuts us off suddenly. Instantly, our training kicks in, and we react without thinking, swerving to escape the danger. In that instant of automatic response, even faster than we can think, our nervous system releases *cortisol.* Within just a couple of seconds our head starts pounding, our stomach starts churning, and everything in our body becomes alert. Our eyesight becomes more focused, our hearing, more sensitive. Even our sense of taste is amplified.

Releasing *cortisol* is like pulling a fire alarm in our nervous system. Every system, every sense in our body goes on high alert. This is good and natural, our body's built-in defense system for responding to real or perceived danger. *Cortisol* is designed to heighten our senses and responsiveness so we can defend ourselves or get ourselves out of a dangerous situation.

Because it is designed for emergencies, *cortisol* is healthy and beneficial in small doses over brief periods of time. Prolonged or frequent secretions of *cortisol*, however, are highly toxic to the body. *Cortisol* is a lethal and highly volatile "high octane" chemical that, in large amounts, fries the immune system. It is a lot like trying to burn high-octane race car fuel in an ordinary sedan that is not designed for it. The hotter-burning fuel will burn up the pistons. In the same way, *cortisol* will destroy the immune system if secreted for long periods of time. People who spend a lot of time in the high negative emotional quadrant–who are angry, fearful, frustrated, or anxious–often flood their bodies with *cortisol*, weakening their immune system and making them more prone to illness. They are sick more often because their prolonged high negative emotional state almost continually triggers the release of *cortisol* into their system.

This is not speculation or theory, but hard science. Years of research in the field of psychoneuroimmunology, which studies how the body and mind work together to promote wellness and ward off disease, have established a clear link between our emotional state and our physical health. The more negative our state of mind, the less immunity we have from disease. Every day people vote themselves out of a long life because of a weakened immune system due to toxic high emotional negativity that they fail to navigate properly.

Think about all the people who are frustrated at work every day. An increasing number of Americans, particularly senior citizens, live in fear daily, afraid to leave their homes because of crime in their neighborhoods. Continuing concerns over terrorism, particularly since September 11, 2001, has cranked the overall fear level a few notches higher for many Americans. Troubled marriages and other relationship problems trigger *high negative* responses in the lives of those involved, particularly women. By a margin of almost three-to-one, women have greater difficulty than men in this area because they are so emotionally connected. Relationship trouble is one of the top stressors in a woman's life.

When our immune system becomes weak or compromised, many things start to go wrong. We become susceptible to all sorts of illnesses and conditions. Even cancer is essentially a by-product of a weakened immune system. Cancer kills, but weakened immunity is what makes us susceptible to cancer in the first place. A strong and healthy immune system wards off most diseases, including cancer.

Immunity is everything to disease or wellness. Prolonged or frequent high emotional negativity triggers the release of *cortisol* which, over time, weakens our immune system and opens us up to disease. That is why it is so critical that we learn how to recognize when we are in a negative emotional state and know how to transition out of it *quickly*.

Breath of Life

As I said before, there are many ways to recover and move from the negative to the positive emotional quadrants, but the quickest way of all is through breathing. I know that sounds very simple, so let me explain. Breath and emotions are interconnected, just as energy levels and emotions are. The word *breathe* literally means "to inspire." In the creation story in the Bible's Book of Genesis, God breathes the breath of life into the nostrils of the first man, and he becomes a living being. Literally, God "inspires" him, and he sits up, full of life. The breath of life fills every organ, cell, and tissue in his body.

The corporate world focuses a lot on motivation, and sometimes confuses it with inspiration. Motivation comes and goes, but inspiration remains. The difference lies in their source. Motivation comes from the outside, but inspiration comes from the inside. Because it so often depends on external circumstances which can change quickly, motivation does not last. Inspiration does. A person who is inspired can keep going long after motivation has waned, because inspiration is an inner drive or force that is not subject to external circumstances.

The opposite of inspiration is expiration. Expiration suggests death or perishing or obsolescence. We put expiration dates on perishable foods such as milk, bread, and meat. Medicines expire after a certain point and lose their effectiveness. Most manufactured goods have a finite shelf life. In the daily scheme of things, we are by the way we live either an inspiration to people or an expiration. Figuratively speaking, we either give life or we give death. When we live positively, we inspire others to positive living. By living negatively, however, we put expiration dates on our own lives and on those who we influence. Think about it. What happens to people in the presence of an inspiring leader? They become energized, pumped, and ready to take on the world. On the other hand, people under the "leadership" of a negative naysayer become listless, pessimistic, and unmotivated. Morale plummets and hope fades.

Breath (inspiration), then, is very important. Breathing is the first thing we do after the womb and the last thing we do before the tomb. It is paramount to our existence. We need oxygen every moment of every day of our lives. Without breathing, we can only live for about two minutes without suffering oxygen depletion and the onset of brain damage.

As important as breath is to life, in our minds we rarely connect it with our emotions. Breath and emotions are inseparably interconnected. What this means is that each quadrant of the emotional navigram has its own characteristic breath pattern, its own unique breath "print" that unmistakably identifies it. Just as each quadrant is different in emotion and energy level, each is also different in *oxygen* level.

In sports science, fitness is defined by the speed at which oxygen is transferred from the lungs to the muscles and blood cells of the body. The faster the rate of oxygen transfer, the more fit the individual. This rate can be measured using a machine called a VO2 Max. Essentially a stationary bicycle, the VO2 Max records cardiopulmonary response. A person being tested mounts the bicycle and is hooked up to a heart monitor that is connected to a computer. The subject's nose is then pinched closed with a plastic pin. During the test the subject breathes into a diving gear-type breathing apparatus that is hooked up to the same computer as the heart monitor. In this way the computer will record heart and oxygen information at the same time, and then relate the two.

Beginning at zero, or resting heart rate, the subject is brought gradually up to 20 minutes of full-blown stress. Afterwards, the data recorded by the computer is analyzed to determine how quickly, and therefore how efficiently, the subject's body can oxygenate blood, particularly under high stress. An out-of-shape individual will have a low VO2 Max score, indicating difficulty in transporting oxygen fast enough for the body's physical demands. Under stress, the body demands oxygen at a rate faster than the pulmonary system can supply it. The more fit an individual, the higher his or her VO2 Max, meaning that the cardio and pulmonary systems are operating more in sync with each other.

What does all this have to do with the relationship between breathing and emotional recovery? It is really very simple. Out of all the different methods for recovery and transition–walking, taking a break, listening to music, laughing, etc.–breathing is the quickest because breath is tied to physiology.

Performance and Recovery

Quick recovery is important because of its relationship to performance. *Performance is measured in the speed of recovery.* The quicker we can recover from a setback, the healthier we are *mentally, emotionally, spiritually,* and *physically.* What matters is not what happens to us but how we respond to what happens to us. Performance is more than just the final score or the bottom line. It also includes how we handle the stress, the bumps, the ups and downs, and the pluses and minuses that happen along the way. Setbacks will occur and storms will come; they are inevitable. The question is, how quickly do we overcome the setback and move on? How swiftly do we pass through the storm and emerge balanced and intact on the other side? When something in life trips you up, what do you do? Do you get all bent out of shape and fret and rail, or do you blow it off and keep going?

Tiger Woods, inarguably one of the best golfers in a generation, has made just as many poor shots as anybody else. One of the qualities that sets him above so many others in his sport is his incredible ability to recover from them so quickly. He can walk into the woods, find his ball, hit it as if he was teeing off, and place it right next to the pin. Tiger Woods has learned how to blow off his bad shots and not become a head case. Instead, he keeps his focus, stays in the "zone" through alignment, and follows up a poor shot with one that puts the ball exactly where he wants it to be. That's what we mean about *speed of recovery* as the measure of performance.

It is the same way in life. Setbacks are not the issue. The issue is how quickly we can recover from them. It doesn't matter what has happened or where we are on the negative side of the navigram. The question we must ask is, what are we doing to get past it? Are we dealing with it or simply ignoring it, hoping it will go away with time? Most people try to ignore it, but to do so is to ignore a ticking time bomb. Unresolved negative emotions eventually become toxic, not only *physically* and *emotionally*, but *mentally* and *spiritually* as well. *Performance (not to mention health) is measured by the speed of recovery.*

Speedy recovery depends in part on our knowing our own limits. For example, there is a big difference between pain and injury. Athletes know their bodies very well. They know when they are in shape and when they are not. They also know when they are injured and when they are merely in pain. By itself, pain can be a good thing because the beginning threshold of pain is that stimulus of stress that allows us to grow in a particular capacity, whether *mentally*, *emotionally*, *spiritually*, or *physically*. The goal of training is growth in capacity, and growth never occurs without some pain.

It always hurts to stretch, at first, but stretching is the only way to lengthen our reach. If we want to stretch and increase our mental capacity, that means we must read and study more. If we want to increase our emotional capacity, that means we have to work hard at being more tolerant with other people, opening ourselves up, risk being vulnerable and transparent, and so forth. If we stop working out the moment we feel pain, we will never accomplish anything. By cautiously pushing through the pain, however, we will see the eventual result of stronger muscles. What we have to watch out for is severe or prolonged pain, which can transition very quickly into injury. That's when we must stop immediately and seek help.

In every area of life, it is very important for us to know the difference between pain and injury. Pain is the threshold to increased capacity, because stress is the stimulus for all growth. Remember that the first marker for *life toughness* is to be *strong*. The only way to become strong is by enduring pain.

EMOTIONAL BREATH PRINTS

Emotionally, as with every other zone, we need to understand our limits. First, we need to know which quadrant we are in and, second, what to do about it. Speedy recovery is our goal because that is what measures our performance. Breathing is the fastest way to recover emotionally because breath is tied to our physiology. However we breathe, our physiology will follow. Each emotional quadrant has its own distinct "breath print." The quickest way to bring our physiology and our emotions into a particular quadrant is by deliberately breathing according to the "breath print" of that quadrant.

The breath print of the *high positive* quadrant is a fast, *deep* breath in and a *fast* breath out, in through the nose and out through the mouth. *Low positive* is also a *deep* breath in, but a *slow* breath out. It is a relaxing, calming breath. *Low negative* is a *shallow* breath in and a *slow* breath out, the breath of a sigh. The breath print for the *high negative* quadrant is a *shallow* breath in and a *fast* breath out. This is the breathing of hyperventilation.

Whatever quadrant we are in emotionally, we breathe according to the breath print of that quadrant; it is natural; it is physiological. When we are excited or pumped, we breathe in deeply and breathe out quickly; when calm and relaxed, we breathe in and out slowly and deeply. If we are sad or depressed, our breathing is shallow in and slow out; if angry or afraid, our breaths are shallow and quick.

The fastest way to change emotional quadrants is by breathing according to the breath print of the quadrant where we want to go. For example, if we are in the high negative quadrant–angry or fearful–and want to move to the positive side, the quickest way is to take two or three *high positive* breaths: *deep* in through the nose and *fast* out through the mouth. What that does is transport enough oxygen into our blood so that our system interprets that we are moving in that direction physiologically. Our emotions *have* to follow because emotions and breath are interconnected. One goes where the other goes.

Anyone who suffers from a panic disorder *lives* in the high negative quadrant. It doesn't take much to set them off into a pattern of quick, shallow breaths, which lead rapidly to hyperventilation, and then everything goes to pieces: thoughts, emotions, behavior. The quickest way to transition someone who is having a panic attack is to help them take two to three deep breaths to get them back on the positive side physiologically and emotionally.

I fly two or three times a week, and every now and then a call is made on the plane for a doctor. On one occasion, when I was on my way home to West Palm Beach from New York, the call came while we were still sitting on the runway at LaGuardia Airport. "Is there a doctor on board?" One woman who was a nurse got up and I got up, and we walked to the back of the cabin where a female passenger was having a panic attack. She was seated in one of the back rows and was freaking out, screaming, "We're going to die! We're going to die! This plane is going to crash!" Five rows of passengers nearby were starting to get nervous, fearing that she might be right. There was pandemonium in the back of that aircraft.

I immediately got on my knees in front of this woman, made eye contact with her, and said, "Look at me. *Breathe* with me." I didn't want to talk to her about her childhood. I didn't need to know if she was on Xanax or not. This was not the time. I had to get her out of the high negative quadrant first. "Look at me. *Breathe* with me." I began to breathe deeply and slowly, and had her match me breath for breath. After three or four of those deep breaths, she was calm. *Now* I could talk to her and find out if she was on medication or if something else was going on.

Breath is connected to emotion. If our emotions are going crazy, the quickest way to bring them under control is to *breathe* from the quadrant where we want them to go.

DICTATORSHIP OR LEADERSHIP?

There is another way to interpret the emotional navigram that has significance for our performance and recovery. Below is the same navigram with the same four quadrants as before, but some additional terms have been added. The two upper quadrants represent performance, while the two lower quadrants represent rest and recovery. As before, the two quadrants on the right are positive and the two on the left, negative.

Performance

Dictate	**Lead**
Angry	Excited
Fearful	Connected
Frustrated	Challenged
Anxious	Pumped
Involuntary	**Voluntary**
Sad	Calm
Depressed	Peaceful
Lonely	Relaxed
Exhausted	Recharged

Rest/Recovery

Dictatorship rules from the high negative quadrant. Fear, anxiety, anger, hostility–all of these are weapons that dictators use to control the people under them. *Leadership*, on the other hand, arises from the high positive quadrant. Effective leaders do not dictate to their people; they *challenge* them. The high negative is a *threat*. The high positive is a *challenge*. A dictator says, "Either you improve, or I'll fire you." A leader addresses a problem with a challenge: "If you improve, we can work together as a team. You can work toward a raise. You can work toward advancement."

Dictators don't care about challenging their people. All they are interested in is controlling others and having their own way. They will not tolerate dissent in the ranks. One of the most memorable images of the 1991 Persian Gulf War for me was the sight of Iraqi soldiers surrendering by the thousands in the desert. Why? They saw an opportunity to get away from a ruthless dictator, and they took it. A dictator's influence extends only as far as his arm can reach or his bullet can travel. Because he rules by threat, he commands very little true loyalty. In order to survive, dictatorship requires the presence of the dictator.

Leadership is different because it operates on principle rather than presence. Those Iraqi soldiers would have willingly died on those sand dunes if they had had a leader they believed in. Leaders do not have to be physically present to have influence, because leadership inspires, and inspiration is eternal. Dictators impose external motivation that disappears as soon as the dictator is out of range. Leaders, however, inspire loyalty and continued high performance because inspiration arises from within and lasts.

Voluntary or Involuntary Recovery?

The lower two quadrants of the navigram represent rest and recovery. On the lower right is the low positive side, or *voluntary recovery.* This means that we go there with a definite plan to "recharge our batteries." Voluntary recovery means being proactive about our need for recovery–thinking about it and planning ahead, even before we need it. Consistent peak performance *under pressure, on demand* occurs only when there is also consistent deliberate periodic recovery. Ideally, recovery should occur every 90 minutes to two hours throughout the day. No matter what our job or schedule, we need to *plan* for regular times when we can relax, be calm, and have a change of pace. Planning for recovery is like keeping tabs on the charge level of our cell phone so we can recharge the battery before it runs down.

The low negative side of the navigram is the zone of *involuntary recovery.* This is where we eventually end up if we don't take voluntary recovery. What goes up must come down. No one can stay in the high quadrants indefinitely. Recovery *will* come. The question is whether we will be proactive in choosing voluntary recovery, or wait until gravity slams us into involuntary recovery.

How many people plan at the beginning of the year to end up on antidepressants in three months? How many establish New Year's resolutions to be drug addicts by the end of the year? Why, then, does it happen? Why are so many people becoming depressed? Why do so many live in a constant state of exhaustion? Many people end up in the low negative quadrant of involuntary recovery simply because they *don't* have a plan *not* to go there.

If we are performing all the time and exerting all this energy, eventually we *will* come down on one side or the other. Through training and planning, we can choose to come down on the positive side. Otherwise, natural forces will pull us down into the negative side. We all need recovery every 90 minutes. Ultimately, we can't live without it. Voluntary recovery is a healthy choice. Involuntary recovery is like a reflex. We can take the strain only so long before that reflex snaps us into the low negative zone of involuntary recovery, leaving us sad, depressed, and exhausted. We didn't plan not to go there, and that is why we ended up there.

Theodore Roosevelt said, "Do what you can, with what you have, where you are." That is all any of us can do. We are limited to whatever resources we have at any given time, and we can't be in two places at once. We *can*, however, be at our best consistently *where* we are, using what we have.

I found this to be so true in my visits to Ground Zero in New York. The needs were so great; so many people needed help. I wanted to be everywhere at once, helping everyone, but I couldn't. I had to remind myself to do what I could with what I had where I was. In Chapter One I related how I broke down emotionally after returning home from Ground Zero the first time. Poor Beemer's head was soaked from my tears. I had held up for so long, trying to get frequent times for my own recovery even as I helped others with theirs. My arrival home was the first time in a week that I had been able to let my guard down, and when I did, everything collapsed. I bawled like a baby. The strain of the week had finally taken its toll, and the weight of it all dragged me down into involuntary recovery.

On the Ceiling

Let's try a couple of exercises. The first one, called "On the Ceiling," is an exercise used in the field for trauma victims as well as in sports science to detach people from negative emotion through mental imagery. By this means we can unplug emotions for a period of time. For many people with deep trauma or anxiety issues, simple recovery breathing is insufficient because of the depth of their problems and the fact that their body chemistry is constantly returning them to the high negative, so they have to focus all the time on breathing. The "On the Ceiling" exercise takes them deeper, and can be used over and over again.

Because of the way our brains are wired, we associate specific emotions with mental pictures, experiences, and memories. Emotions are neutral and must be tied to something, or the results could be disastrous. Electricity is beneficial and useful as long as it flows through a circuit in a controlled manner. Uncontrolled electricity is explosive and deadly. Lightning is a good example. Our emotions are the same way; they must be harnessed and attached to something.

Traumatic personal experiences–rape, for example–often leave vivid images imprinted in the mind, images that have high negative emotions attached to them. Such experiences can cause the brain to become cross-wired, as it were, leaving the victim with severe anxiety disorders. Any word or event that the victim in any way associates with the traumatic experience stimulates a strong and highly negative emotional response. Something must be done to help this person dissociate their unhealthy negative emotions from their mental images of the event. The "On the Ceiling" exercise helps them do this.

Here's how it works. Get comfortable and close your eyes. With your eyes closed, think of a situation or an experience that you have had that put you into the high negative emotional quadrant–something that made you very angry, frightened, or anxious. Take a minute or two to get that event solidly fixed in your mind. Imagine it as though it has just happened, and is still very fresh. See it, smell it, taste it, and feel it. In your mind, put yourself back in that situation. Remember not only the event itself, but also how you felt. On a scale of 1-10, with 1 low and 10 high, where are you emotionally as you picture this event? Be honest with yourself.

Now, step out of yourself and to the side, looking back as if you are watching yourself experience this event on a television screen about ten or twelve paces away. Again, on a scale of 1-10, where are you emotionally? Now, move farther away and imagine yourself on the ceiling about 25 or 30 feet high, looking down on yourself in that situation. Once again, monitor your emotions on that scale of 1-10. Where are you now emotionally?

Did you find that your emotional response became less intense the farther away you moved from the situation in your mind? The more we learn to dissociate ourselves mentally from traumatic experiences—the more detached we can become—the less intense the emotional responses we attach to those images will become. This is very powerful, because *what our mind sees, our physiology believes*. If we can pull away mentally from a bad experience, our emotions will follow.

This exercise works because it first puts us into direct association with the strong negative emotions attached to the experience. Stepping off to the side and going up on the ceiling basically helps dissociate us from that situation, essentially making us a third party observer rather than a participant. All of a sudden, our emotions settle out and we say, "Okay, I'm not over there, I'm over *here*." We get so far away from that experience that we "unplug" the emotion associated with it.

Recovery and Performance Snapshots

The second exercise involves taking two mental "snapshots," just as with a camera.

Look at the two boxes below. On the left is the "Rest/Recovery" snapshot, and on the right, the "Zone Performance" snapshot. First, think of a place or an activity that appeals to you and in which you would be completely relaxed. Maybe for you it is the beach, or a walk in the woods. Maybe going parasailing would relax you. For me, it is resting in a hammock between two palm trees on the island of Fiji. Whatever it is for you, imagine it clearly. Now, draw a picture of it in the "Rest/Recovery" box. This is an image that represents the low positive, voluntary recovery quadrant where we want to go for recovery.

Rest/Recovery Snapshot	**Zone Performance Snapshot**

Next, imagine an activity that puts you into the high positive quadrant–something that really pumps you and gets you excited and energized. For many people, this equates to that which gives them the greatest fulfillment or sense of purpose in life. For me, it is speaking and teaching on stage in front of thousands of people. What is it for you? Do you have a picture of it in your mind? Now draw it in the "Zone Performance" box.

Here is the significance of these two "snapshots." We all need a low positive association picture so that when we are burning on all cylinders and need some speedy recovery, the "Rest/Recovery" snapshot can help us move to that place quickly, just by imagining it. Our best performance usually comes out of the high positive quadrant, and the "Zone Performance" snapshot helps us move there quickly by associating it in our minds with something that we love, something that excites us and pumps us up just by doing it. Whether we need to think performance as the pressure comes on, or recovery after performing, these two "snapshots" will help us be able to move into either of the two positive quadrants at will.

Chapter Five

Radar Navigation

Every now and then, somewhere, some place, sometime, you are going to have to plant your feet, stand firm, and make a point about who you are and what you believe in. When that time comes, Pat, you simply have to do it.

—Lee Riley (father of NBA coach Pat Riley)

Dick and Ricky Hoyt are a father-son team who has participated together in over 700 competitions. One time they even cycled across America together. In 1999, at the time of their final "Ironman" competition, Dick was 59 and Ricky, a full-grown young man. Held annually in Hawaii, the "Ironman" is a daylong event that begins with a 2½-mile swim, followed by a 112-mile bicycle race, and culminating in a 26.2-mile marathon. During the bicycle portion of the race, the effect of the wind on their combined weight was very taxing for Dick. In addition, the Hoyts' bicycle developed a problem with its brakes. By the time they got it fixed, they were too late to make the cut-off time. With now no chance of winning, Dick and Ricky had to finish the last 63 miles for each other.

Here's the kicker: Ricky Hoyt was born with cerebral palsy. He cannot walk and speaks only with difficulty. Yet inside his chest beats the heart of a champion and a true competitor. Ricky lives in his own apartment, has a degree in special education from Boston College, and believes that persons with disabilities should be able to live and be included in regular daily activities just like everyone else.

When swimming, Dick pulls Ricky behind him; when cycling, Ricky occupies a special seat in the front while Dick pedals. Dick regards his son as the true competitor, the one who inspires him to push for his best. When he is pushing Ricky, Dick says, something rises in him that enables him to go faster and do more; something that he can't quite explain. For his part, Ricky says that when his father is pulling him in the water or pushing him on the bicycle are the times he feels the most normal.

Here are two individuals who have connected with the spiritual side of their lives, who have discovered what animates them and makes them who they are. They believe in each other so much, and in their competing together, that they are willing to sacrifice to that extreme, just to win a race. At heart, however, this has nothing to do with a race, but everything to do with their *life purpose*.

Life Purpose

What in your life do you want *so* much that you would work *that* hard for it? What do you believe in so strongly that it becomes the central focus of your life, your reason for being? Why are you alive? What is your purpose for being on the planet? When we talk about *life purpose*, we are talking about *passion release*, that which stirs up and unleashes the passion in our spirit. Finding our *life purpose* involves discovering what we are truly passionate about—that which *inspires* us and is the driving force of our life.

Life purpose relates to the *spiritual* zone of our being. Our spiritual acuity moves beyond the mechanics of life—the "how-tos"—to touch on the *why* of life. In our analogy of navigating an aircraft through a storm, the *spiritual* zone is represented by the radar system. Radar navigation gives a pilot the "big picture" so that he is fully aware of the surrounding environment. A pilot needs a clear picture of where he is so he can know how to get where he wants to go. In the same way, the *spiritual* zone keeps us in touch with the big picture of who we are, where we are, where we have come from, and where we are going.

Our *life purpose* is tied closely to what we *believe*. Our English word "believe" derives from the Greek word *pisteuo*, which literally means "to cling to, to hang on to with all our might." Imagine yourself hanging onto a rope over the edge of a high cliff. How much faith do you have in that rope? To what percentage do you *believe* in that rope? Twenty percent? Fifty percent? Seventy-five percent? If that rope is the only thing preventing you from falling to the rocks below, you had better believe in it one hundred percent. That kind of belief involves *total commitment*. Our *life purpose* is shaped and defined by those beliefs that we hold so strongly that we are willing to stake our life on them.

What is your rope? What are the strands of belief that make your rope what it is? The Bible says that a cord of three strands is not easily broken. It is referring to the strands of relationships with God, self, and others. What are the strands of your rope? For me personally, they are God, family, and country. I am a Christian. My personal relationship with God is very important to me and helps me every day in navigating life.

Life purpose can and does relate to our religious beliefs, whatever they may be, but it involves more than that. It doesn't necessarily have to be defined only in terms of religious faith. What defines our *life purpose* is that which animates our spirit, that from which we derive meaning and fulfillment in life. We all need an anchor for our soul, something to tie ourselves to that will hold us firm and steady through the buffeting storms of life.

A fulfilled life is a life lived with the big picture always in view. The radar screen on an aircraft will show us where we are and what is all around us, but it cannot show us *why* we are on the journey. The *why* of life must come from within. Each of us must determine for ourselves why we are here and what we should be doing. That is why our personal belief system is so very important. It is paramount to what we do every day. What we believe in lies behind our passion, our inspiration, our motivation, and even our ability to persevere, to stay the course and keep coming back until we prevail. Our beliefs give us purpose and help us answer the question of why we are alive.

So often we fly through life without thinking about the big picture. We live from day to day and week to week with no clear end in mind. We have no clear plan of action for life and do not think through in advance the possible consequences of our actions. This is one reason why so many times we shoot ourselves in the foot by making ill-considered or unhealthy decisions.

I do training in middle schools and high schools, and one thing I always try to impress upon the students is the danger and potential tragedy of making an improper decision from the wrong emotional quadrant. At the same time, I stress the value and power of correct decisions made from a condition of proper spiritual alignment. When we know why we are alive and what our *life purpose* is, it is easier to make plans and decisions that serve and advance that purpose.

The two big questions of life are *how?* and *why?* Of the two, *how?* is easier to answer than *why?* because *why?* can consist of so many different flavors and variations. The *how?* of life usually has a tangible answer. The *why?* of life, on the other hand, is intangible. Passion, motivation, perseverance, force, inspiration, and strength all flow from the *why?* of life.

It is interesting to note that during preseason training, *every* NFL team is going to the Super Bowl. No team goes into the season setting its sights on winning only a few games or only taking its division. They plan to go all the way to the top. Coaches commonly try to inspire and motivate their players by keeping the big picture before them–believing in that dream and keeping their eyes on the big prize to help players remember why they get up each morning, why they put on those pads and helmets, and why they endure the endless drills and brutal physical punishment of the training camp.

The problem starts a few weeks into the season when the win/loss statistics have started to take shape across the league. How do coaches continue to motivate a team that has more losses than wins? They do it the same way as in preseason, by keeping players focused on the end goal: "All we need is a few more wins in our division, and we could be a wild card. We could still make the playoffs, and then anything can happen." Then they will start telling stories of teams who overcame great odds to win the championship.

That may be fine in sports, but what about our everyday lives at work and at home? How do we stay focused on the big picture? What do we have to do to wake up and get pumped and inspired and ready to make a difference in our world? It is a matter of homing in on our life purpose through "radar navigation"—spiritual or purpose alignment.

Purpose Alignment

When we are in touch with our *life purpose,* that purpose will manifest itself in our lives by at least four specific characteristics: *passion, motivation, perseverance,* and *force.* By "force" I mean the force or strength necessary to push beyond barriers, overcome obstacles, and prevail. Most people desire these qualities in their lives. Who wants to live a life devoid of passion? What good is a life that is an endless procession of days with no drive other than just to get by? Without passion and motivation there is little drive either to persevere or to press forward.

As desirable as these traits are, many of us have great difficulty experiencing them on any consistent basis. The main problem is that we have everything backwards. If we try to "find" passion or motivation we will be disappointed. If we try to "get" perseverance and force, we will fail. These things are not the path to purpose alignment; they are by-products of purpose alignment. Alignment of purpose must come first, and then these others will flow from that alignment. An illustration here will help explain.

PURPOSE CHART

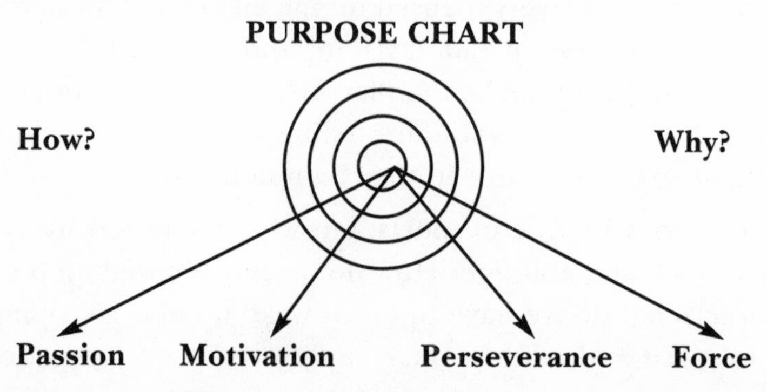

In this "Purpose Chart," the concentric circles represent a target. The bull's-eye in the center represents our *life purpose*, that which fills our life with meaning and significance and stimulates us to get out of bed every day. We could also call it a *purpose release trigger*. Whenever that trigger is pressed, it releases *passion*, *motivation*, *perseverance*, and *force*. On the chart, notice how the four arrows point *outward* from the bull's-eye rather than point toward it. *Passion*, *motivation*, *perseverance*, and *force* are *by-products* of a purpose-aligned life.

We cannot sustain passion. We cannot sustain motivation. Instead, we must find out what we are already aligned to—what our *purpose release trigger* is—and focus on it. For Dick and Ricky Hoyt, it was each other. For me, that bull's-eye is my relationship with God, which defines my life. Out of that definition come my family and my career. A real *purpose release trigger* for me is my son Brandon. Whenever I think about him, passion and motivation really start flowing through me. I get all pumped up very quickly and feel like I could go through a wall for him.

Everybody needs a purpose in life. It is important that we understand what drives us. A wise proverb in the Bible says that without vision, people perish. We have to have a vision of where our life is going or we will end up nowhere. Lack of *passion*, *motivation*, the *perseverance* to keep going, or the *force* to push through difficult things, are symptoms of a deeper problem. The real issue is impotent purpose, which is nothing more than a small vision or picture of who we are and what we should be doing. Big vision means big passion; big vision means big motivation. If we are correctly aligned with our purpose, then *passion*, *motivation*, *perseverance*, and *force* will flow forth as by-products.

ID Badge

Let's try another exercise. I use this routinely in training to help people begin to get a handle on identifying their *life purpose*. It's called the *ID Badge*. The goal of the exercise is for each person to describe his or her *life purpose* in three words or less. This is not as easy as it may sound at first, because very few of us have ever tried to define the meaning of our life in such concise terms. For this reason, I usually begin with something a little broader. Here's how it works.

First, take a piece of paper and a pencil, and *in one sentence* describe *who you are* and *what you do*. Who you are means more than just your name. What defines *you* as a person? How would you describe yourself? There is more to *what you do* than simply your job or career. *Why* do you do what you do? Is there a larger purpose beyond simply bringing home a paycheck? Think about it for a couple of minutes, then write down your self-description in one sentence.

Now, examine your one-sentence description and pull out no more than three key words that define you even more precisely. Write them down. You may wish to use the space below. These key words make up your ID Badge.

What words best describe who you are? Focus on adjectives rather than nouns; words like "passionate," or "outgoing," or "exciting." You get the idea. Second, what words best describe what you do, what fires you up and gives your life meaning. The basic purpose of the ID Badge is for you to define what makes you who you are. What makes you unique as a person that you would want someone else to know? Your ID Badge should define you in such a way that anyone who knows you could look at your badge and say, "Yes, that's you."

ID Badge

Do you need some help? My ID Badge is "Life Coach." That defines what I do. Professionally, I train people in how to navigate life's storms successfully. Therefore, I am a "life coach." When I do this exercise in training seminars, people have a lot of fun with it and come up with some really creative responses. Someone might describe herself as a "passionate accounts person." One man who was a manager in a company wrote as his ID Badge, "Professional Babysitter." Serious or lighthearted, it doesn't matter; your ID Badge can say anything as long as it truly defines you.

Our ID Badge is useful in two ways. First, it helps other people understand who we are and why we do what we do. Second, it reminds us of the same thing. There are days when things are going rough and it is easy to forget who I am; to lose sight of my purpose. All I have to do is look at my own badge and say, "Oh yes, *this* is what I am called to do." There are times when we don't feel like sticking it through and doing what we are supposed to, but have little choice. We simply have to suck it up and do it. Keeping our ID Badge at hand can help us remember our *life purpose* and help us keep our focus so that we can carry out our *purpose alignment*, thereby keeping *passion*, *motivation*, *perseverance*, and *force* flowing even under less than ideal circumstances.

VALUES AND PURPOSE

One very important benefit of correct *purpose alignment* is that it helps us maintain the proper connection between our *values* and our *purpose*. Values and purpose are not the same, but they are related. Interestingly enough, although many psychologists and other professionals in the field of mental health and behavior, both past and present, have studied and written about both values and purpose, it seems that few of them have made the connection between the two.

For many years it was a mystery to me how good people with solid, positive values could make foolish and unhealthy decisions. Nevertheless, it happens all the time. In the course of my own studies I learned that a fundamental relationship exists between our system of values and our sense of purpose. When everything functions as it should, our *values* shape our *life purpose*, and the way we live out our *life purpose* reflects our values. Sometimes, however, we make decisions that run contrary to the values we claim to hold, and are at odds with our professed life purpose. This usually means that some sort of disconnect has occurred in the alignment of our *purpose* and our *values*. For whatever reason, we don't relate what we *do* to what we *believe*.

To a large degree, this values/purpose relationship is a natural characteristic of brain chemistry and function. Each hemisphere of the brain, left and right, is responsible for specific functions that are related, yet different. The illustration below will help us visualize this.

Values
Left Brain

80% Speech
Sequential Order
Logic
Time Cognition
Data

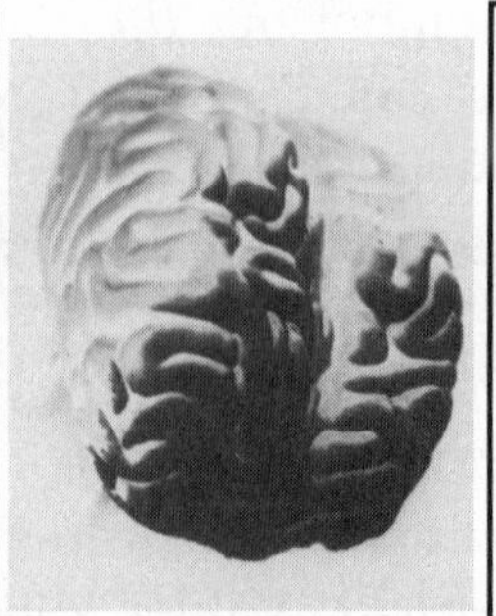

Purpose
Right Brain

20% Speech
Visual Spatial
No Logic
Passion/Purpose
Music

Eighty percent of our capacity for speech comes from the left brain. Sequential ordering is found there as well. That is our ability to put things in sequence: 1, 2, 3, 4; a, b, c, d; etc. Logic is also a function of the left brain, as is time cognition.

The left brain is also the primary data storage facility. One of the main operations of the left brain is the processing of information. It takes it apart, looks at it, and analyzes the data stored.

The right brain has a very different function. First of all, only 20 percent of our speech comes from the right brain. That is just enough speech for the right brain to interpret what the left brain sends across the corpus callosum, the membrane that connects the two hemispheres of the brain. Without some speech function, the right brain would be a dormant hemisphere. Visual spatial capacity—an aerial view of life—is housed in the right brain. No logic is found there, however. In the right brain, nothing has to make sense; the left brain takes care of that. The right brain has no sense of time. It doesn't care how late or how early we are or how long or how short we stay. *Passion*, *motivation*, *perseverance*, and *force* all emanate from the right brain. It is also where we get our ability to understand and appreciate music and the other arts.

Another way to describe the two hemispheres of the brain is to say that the left hemisphere is the more logical, factual, and orderly side, while the right hemisphere is the more emotional, creative, and spontaneous side. A critical part of the alignment process is getting these two sides of the brain working in concert with each other, rather than at cross-purposes.

Here is an example. I read a great deal in my work, much of it while traveling. One technique that helps my retention level is to listen to music while I read. Reading to learn and retain factual data is a left-brain activity. Listening to music stimulates the right brain, where creativity is centered, prompting the visual spatial capacity to create a mental picture in response to the music. When the data collection of the left brain from the reading is connected with a picture from the right brain aroused more readily by the music, the result is greatly increased recall.

In their respective and distinct functions, the left and right hemispheres of the brain complement and enhance each other in an interdependent relationship. Because of this interdependence, and in spite of what several generations of parents have told their children, young people really *can* listen to music and do homework at the same time. The right brain activity of listening to the music actually helps them relax and visualize to better retain the factual, logical, and sequentially ordered data they are studying with their left brain.

As I studied this left brain-right brain relationship, one day it hit me that this is also how values and purpose relate to each other. Our *values* are a *left-brain* function. *Purpose* is *right brain*. Values have to do with knowledge and information, while purpose deals with vision. A biblical proverb says that without vision, people perish. Our vision capability is located in the visual cortex in the back lobe of our brain. What does vision do for us? It gives us a perspective or perception of an image; it gives us a *picture*. Stating the proverb another way, without a *picture*, people perish. In other words, we have to be able to *see* where we are going.

Purpose alignment helps us mesh together our left and right brain functions into a coordinated whole, thus linking our values and behavior with our purpose. People with good values sometimes make unhealthy decisions because they don't have their values connected to their picture or vision of life.

Programming Your VCR

Failure to make our purpose alignment can lead us in the wrong direction and leave us with a skewed sense of priorities. Several years ago, I gained some significant insight into this issue. As is so often the case with me, this insight came in the context of my relationship with my son Brandon.

Because of his condition, Brandon is able to do nothing on his own, but one of the things he loves is watching television. Consequently, we have literally hundreds of videotapes of all different kinds: home videos, ball games, bowling, racing, cartoons, etc. On any given day we will put some tapes in and let him watch for awhile. Then we will play with him and do some things as a family. Later, Brandon will go back in his room and watch television some more. Even with the mind of a five-year-old, Brandon is still 18 and likes his space.

Since Brandon cannot talk, one of the challenges is knowing which video he wants to watch. Often it is trial and error. I will put a tape in the VCR and watch Brandon's face. If he gets excited, I know I chose the right one. If his face shows disappointment, I know I need to choose another tape. I will pull the first one out, then try a different one. This can go on for quite some time before I find the one Brandon wants to watch.

One day, as I was engaged in putting tapes in and pulling them out trying to find the right one for Brandon to watch, I started thinking, "What if life was like a VCR, that we could manipulate at will? After all, what are the options with a VCR? We can play, rewind, fast-forward, eject, tape over a previous recording, or even throw a tape away." That's when it came, one of those insights I like to call a "God-moment." It was suddenly so clear: VCR: **V**alues, **C**haracter, **R**eputation.

All of us have an image, a picture of ourselves that we present to the world. By itself, an image is neutral; it takes on specific qualities according to the values and character with which we endow it. Whether we present a positive image or a negative image depends on where we start in the lineup and in which direction we move. Look at the illustration below.

V C R

Values Character Reputation

V C R for a positive image

R C V for a negative image

Beginning with values and moving toward reputation will produce a positive and healthy image. When we have a set of *values* that we believe in and adhere to, over time, those *values* produce *character* in us, and *character*, over time, leaves behind a *reputation*. People don't see our values; they see our character. Our values are internal and invisible, but our character is external and on display. In a sense, our character is the outward manifestation—the "skin," if you will—of the values hidden inside of us. Values lived out constitute character, which leads to a positive or a negative reputation.

Reputation is designed to be long-term, but it can only be healthy over a period of time if lived out consistently one day at a time. We should not have to be concerned about our reputation. Instead, we should be concerned about our character, which derives from and reflects our values. This is where many people, particularly young people, get messed up. If we *start* with concern for our reputation, and move in the opposite direction toward values, we run into trouble. Our reputation becomes more important to us than anything else. We become fixated on what other people think about us.

Reputation is not what we think about ourselves, but what we think other people think about us. If we are more concerned about our reputation than we are about our values or our character, it means that our character is flawed and our values are *situational*. This results in a negative and unhealthy image. Rather than being guided by our values, we make choices based upon who we are with or where we are. Choices made on that basis are usually wrong.

VALUES EVALUATION

Purpose alignment means connecting our values with our vision for ourselves and for the life we want to live. That's why the "Rest/Recovery" and "Zone Performance" snapshots we did in the previous chapter are important. We need clear pictures of what energizes us so that we will know when we are in the zone and doing what we were meant to do. Also, those pictures will make it easier for us to recognize when we are *not* in the zone and are acting contrary to our *life purpose*.

Here is another exercise that I use routinely in training. Below is a list of 12 of the most common values that show up on surveys. While not a comprehensive list, these represent the values that are generally regarded by most Americans as the most important. There may be some values important to you personally that are not on this list; if so, add them to the list.

VALUES

Choose four and prioritize:

Power	**Love**	**Health**	**Passion**
Comfort	**Intimacy**	**Adventure**	**Security**
Success	**Freedom**	**Loyalty**	**Family**

From the list, choose the *four* values that mean the most to *you*. What is most important in your life? If a value not on the list is one of your top four, include it. The point of this exercise is to identify what values you hold most dear. These are the things that energize and animate your life. They should be consistent with the internal vision you have of yourself—the picture of that person you want to be. In other words, your values should support the picture you have of yourself. If you want to become or continue to be the person in that picture, you need to stay in touch with these values.

Now that you have chosen your top four values, prioritize them. Number them from one to four according to the priority of importance which you place on them. Let's say you chose love, health, passion, and family as your four top values. Now, which of those four is most important? Assign it number one. Perhaps love tops your list, followed by passion, then health, and finally, family. Your priority list would look like this: Love–1; Passion–2; Health–3; Family–4. Whatever four you chose, take a couple of minutes now and arrange them according to priority.

Arranging our values according to priority is important because they have a "firing order," just like an automobile engine. If you open the hood of your car and switch out two of the spark plug wires on your engine, the vehicle will not run properly. The firing order is out of sequence. In the same way, our values must "fire" in proper order if we want our desired character to show and leave behind the right kind of reputation.

Writing Your Obituary

Earlier in the chapter I asked you to write out your personal ID Badge that condensed your *life purpose* into three words or less. Now I want you to expand on that a little bit. I want you to write out your obituary. Your obituary is the end result of your ID Badge. What would you want said about you after you are gone? How would you wish to be remembered? In the end, who did you become, and what did you do? Did you live your life consistently with your life purpose? Did you fulfill the vision that was in your heart?

Think about it for a few minutes. Then, in one paragraph, write out your obituary. You may wish to use the space below. If you desire a greater challenge, condense your obituary to an epitaph. If all anyone could ever know about you was what was carved on your tombstone, what would you want it to say?

Your Obituary

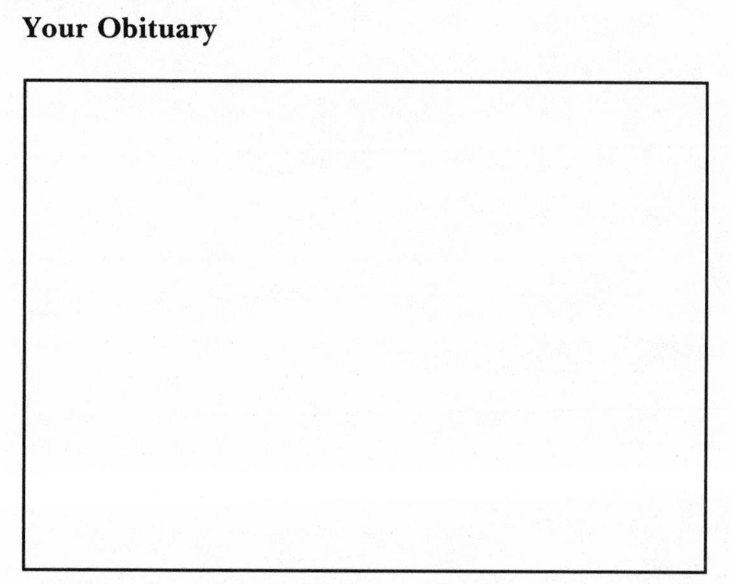

There is a philosophy in the Bible that describes the Word of God as a lamp to our feet and a light to our path. That is an apt analogy for us in talking about vision and purpose. In life we need both short and long vision. Short vision is the lamp to our feet that shows us where we are to step *right now*, in the immediate. Long vision is the light to our path that illuminates the way we should go over the long term. As they relate to understanding our *life purpose*, our ID Badge is the lamp to our feet; it is what we do *today*. Our obituary is the light to our path; thinking with this end in mind, it is what we do and who we become throughout our life.

CHAPTER SIX

VEHICLE NAVIGATION

Power is not revealed by striking hard or often,
but by striking true.

—Honore de Balzac

IN THE FINAL ANALYSIS, NO MATTER how thorough his preparations may be, no pilot can get where he wants to go without an aircraft to fly. He may have a great flight plan, his instruments may work perfectly, and he may have the most sophisticated radar system in the world. Despite these advantages, however, his ultimate success will come down to two things: the physical condition of his aircraft and the quality of its fuel. All the other systems are vital, but it is the aircraft itself—the vehicle—that will physically transport the pilot to his destination. How easily and comfortably he gets there will depend in large measure on how well he takes care of it.

By the same analogy, we have a *physical* vehicle which we use to navigate through life and which contains and transports the *mental*, *emotional*, and *spiritual* parts of our being. Humans are not non-corporeal life-forms with no physical substance. We cannot transport ourselves from one place to another telepathically. We possess physical bodies that, while living, are inseparably integrated with our *mental, emotional,* and *spiritual* capacities. We come as a package: body, mind, and spirit.

As a transport device, our body is a force to be reckoned with. If our body gives out before our mind and spirit do, we will go to our grave with music still in us—unfulfilled potential. I don't know about you, but I don't want to come to the end of my life and look back only to discover that I never became all I could have been, or did all I could have done. *A fulfilled life is doing what we can, with what we have, where we are.* The best way to ensure that we can release the full potential of our *mental, emotional,* and *spiritual* capacities is to give proper care to the vehicle that carries them—our *physical* body.

Building and maintaining a healthy body involves giving attention to four major areas: *nutrition, exercise, hydration,* and *rest and recovery cycles.* Each of these has a direct influence on our energy levels and overall physical health. The more physically fit we are, the more energy we have, and the better able we are to adjust to changing energy levels. Aside from a little basic knowledge in each of these major areas, good physical health is essentially a matter of common sense and moderation.

Body Fuel

For several decades now many Americans have been obsessed with dieting and weight loss. Currently, obesity is at an all-time high in this country. A big part of the problem is that we don't know what to eat or how to eat for optimal health. Considering the constant barrage of information and misinformation that we receive from infomercials, widely-touted diet plans, clinical studies, and advice from so-called "experts," it is not surprising that so many of us are confused about the elements of basic nutrition. Our modern high-tech, fast-lane lifestyle doesn't help either, because it discourages healthy eating habits.

Most diets do not work because they are unsustainable over the long term. A diet is a *program*—a *temporary* solution to an *ongoing* problem—and our bodies are not designed for programs. Our bodies are designed for *lifestyle*. The answer to obesity and other nutrition-related problems is to understand how our bodies are hardwired nutritionally, and to align our habits and lifestyle with that wiring, thus avoiding the bad programming we find in society from so many sources that give us only part of the story.

One example of bad programming that we have to deal with is the long established and widely accepted belief that healthy nutrition means eating *three* square meals a day. The corporate world as a whole has modified this to where many business executives and employees routinely eat no more than twice a day. This is in conflict with our internal wiring. Our bodies are designed to eat *not* two or three times a day, but *five* or *six* times a day. We have a long digestive tract that is conducive to our eating more or less continually throughout the day; optimally, about every three hours.

We should eat every three hours because our bodies regulate our blood sugar levels in three-hour cycles. Every three hours we need some food in our system to help keep our blood sugar in balance. Digesting food raises the level of sugar in our blood, which is necessary for energy and to fuel our bodies. This rise in blood sugar stimulates the pancreas to release insulin, which helps facilitate the rapid transfer of glucose and amino acids from the bloodstream into muscles and other tissues. As glucose passes from the blood into other cells of the body, the blood sugar level decreases once again. Insulin, then, serves also to keep the blood sugar level under control. The entire cycle generally takes three hours. After three hours, blood sugar is at a level sufficiently low that the body needs a fresh supply of fuel to start the cycle over again.

Anyone with Type 2 diabetes understands the importance of this. Type 2 diabetics must have something to eat approximately every three hours or they start having problems. *Mentally*, they begin to lose their ability to concentrate, or to stay focused on anything for very long. *Emotionally*, they become tense and uneasy, sometimes displaying an erratic emotional response to normal circumstances around them. *Spiritually*, they lose sight of why they are doing what they are doing. Whatever *purpose alignment* they may have had goes right out the window. *Physically*, their energy levels plummet, which can leave them feeling light-headed and lead to fainting spells. In extreme cases, they can go into a sugar coma, and possibly even die.

Controlling Type 2 diabetes through diet by eating every three hours is *not* a radical solution. It is merely paying attention to basic physiology and body chemistry. For some reason, however, most people who do not have diabetes assume that this three-hour cycle does not apply to them because their natural insulin levels are still working and regulating their blood sugar.

What Type 2 diabetics do out of necessity, all of us should do by design. Type 2 diabetes is rapidly becoming a health epidemic in this country, having increased 33 percent in the past ten years. Important factors in this increase appear to relate to both the frequency and the quality of our eating.

To keep a fire burning, we have to add more fuel periodically. It is the same way with our body. Human metabolism is a furnace that never goes out. Like any other furnace, it needs a regular supply of fuel to keep burning. If we do not fuel it, it will eventually begin consuming muscle fiber and body tissue. Without food, our body will feed on itself in order to stoke its own stove. That is what happens to many starving people in third world nations. Their stomachs bloat from the buildup of acid and toxicity, and they eventually die as a result of their body consuming itself.

All four of our acuities–*mental*, *emotional*, *spiritual*, and *physical*–are interrelated and interdependent. Food is the fuel that, when processed by the body, provides the energy to keep them all functioning. If our eating habits are out of sync with our physiology, our ability to master our energy levels and perform at peak throughout the day will be greatly hindered. If we don't have the energy level to stay focused and on task, our thoughts will begin to wander. We will become easily distracted and will not put our heart and soul into anything we do. When our body chemistry is messed up, it is impossible for us to be at our best.

One of the quickest ways to increase our performance is to make sure that we are taking in the right kind of body fuel on a *regular* basis. We could think of ourselves as a lean and agile high performance vehicle with a small fuel tank that allows us to run only about three hours between fill-ups. During those three-hour periods we're operating on all cylinders, humming along at peak proficiency. If we try to blow past a refill checkpoint, however, and do it often enough, eventually we will find ourselves out of gas and stranded on the side of the road. We need to respect our physiology and give our body the fuel it needs when it needs it.

NUTRITION

When it comes to matters of basic nutrition for a lifestyle geared for peak performance, there are four simple, commonsense guidelines.

1. *Eat a* **small** *meal or snack every three hours.*

The key to success in this step is found in the word "small." One problem many people have when they first hear the idea of eating six times a day is that they envision meals the same size as what they are already accustomed to eating two or three times a day. Increasing the *frequency* of our eating calls for a subsequent *decrease* in the *quantity* of food that we consume each time we eat. Our primary purpose in eating is to keep our body fueled, and the most efficient way to do that is by feeding it *smaller* portions of food at three-hour intervals.

When I speak of a "small" meal, I am referring to a portion of food sufficient to fill a plate, generous but not heaping. In America, most of us eat two to three times more at one sitting than we need. Our philosophy seems to be that if we eat a big meal now, we won't need to eat again for six or seven hours. Physiologically, however, it doesn't work out that way. A large meal takes much longer for the body to digest and metabolize, and we pay a heavy price in decreased energy levels. Blood rushes from the upper extremities of our body to the stomach to aid in digesting the large amount of food we have consumed. As a result, our body shuts down in order to keep the fires of digestion burning. Our energy level plummets, and our acuities lose their edge.

What athlete would eat heavily right before competing? What performing artist would have a large meal just before going on stage? They know better. One of the quickest ways to limit our performance is to eat a large meal, yet that is just what most of us do. Society has programmed us that way. Physically, we are *wired* to eat small meals five or six times a day, but we are *programmed* to eat large meals two or three times a day. We tell ourselves that it is for convenience, that we don't have time to eat more frequently.

A small meal would be 700-800 calories, with a proper balance between proteins and carbohydrates. A snack would be smaller, perhaps 200-250 calories: a piece of fruit, half of a small bagel, a few pretzels, wheat crackers, a power bar, etc. These are not exact figures by any means. The point here is *not* to count calories, but to hit home the fact that we should eat five or six times a day, including meals and snacks, and that our meals should be smaller than what we are normally accustomed to.

Eating smaller portions with greater frequency is critical for two reasons. First, it enables us to have the energy levels we need to be lean and light throughout the day without getting bogged down by our own body chemistry from overeating. Second, eating more often in smaller amounts through the day keeps our metabolism burning fast, which is always a good thing. As teenagers, most of us could eat anything we wanted and just burn it off, because we had fast metabolism. As we grow older, however, our metabolism naturally slows down. The quickest way to speed it up is by eating frequently in small meals.

When our metabolism burns fast, we burn calories at a higher rate, even when sitting still or sleeping. Fast metabolism means our body is working for us, keeping a pilot light burning all the time. Regardless of how low our stove might get, the pilot light stays on because it knows that we will soon be throwing in more fuel. Eating frequently turns the flame up, which increases the rate of fuel consumption. That's the way our body works.

Simply changing from three large meals a day to five or six small ones can enhance performance significantly. Depending on how many meals a day someone eats, his performance may increase by 10, 20, or even 40 percent.

Because of the way we have been programmed, most of us eat for taste rather than for fuel. Taste is important, but we need to be driven by fuel, not taste. We need to eat in such a way as to get us through each three-hour window efficiently without getting bogged down by out-of-sync body chemistry.

2. *Eat breakfast every day.*

Many people routinely skip breakfast every morning, for all kinds of reasons. They don't have time, they don't like food early in the morning, they are still full from eating too much before bed, etc. In today's fast and frantic corporate world that so frequently seems to allow time for only two meals, breakfast often is regarded as the most expendable. In truth, however, it is probably the most important.

The word breakfast means to "break fast." Our bodies have been fasting through the night as we sleep. Our fuel supply is low, our metabolism has slowed, and our flame has died down. We need food early in the day, shortly after we wake up, simply to jump-start our metabolism and get it going again. If we expect to have the energy and chemical balance we need to work at peak through the day, we must get into the habit of fueling our bodies first thing in the morning. It's important to eat *something* for breakfast, even if it is only a bowl of cereal.

3. *Consume less fat.*

4. *Reduce simple sugars.*

These last two really go together when we are talking about sensible nutrition, particularly in light of the eating habits of so many Americans over the past 10 or 15 years. Throughout the 1990s, Americans as a whole got *fatter* eating *fat-free* food. During that decade, we consumed more *no-fat* and *low-fat* food than at any time in our history, resulting in a 15 to 20 percent per capita increase in obesity. Recent studies have revealed that today, 63 percent of Americans are overweight, with 25 to 30 percent of those classified as medically obese, meaning they are at least 20 percent over their ideal weight.

How did this happen? How did eating *no-fat* and *low-fat* food make us fatter? A lot of it has to do with slick product packaging and marketing, as well as the fact that many of us were not in the habit of reading labels. A general ignorance of where the taste in food comes from was also a factor.

Reducing fat was on everybody's mind, so food processors and packagers met the demand by marketing foods from which the fat had been removed. Had we looked at labels in those days the way we do now, we would have discovered that in place of the fat, these foods contained two to three times as much sugar as the same foods without the fat removed. Taste in food comes from two places: fat and sugar. If the fat is removed, more sugar must be added to compensate in flavor.

Many people assumed that if a food was fat free, it was safe to eat it in large quantities. For example, seeing a large bag of "fat-free" potato chips, they would think, "Hey, this is fat-free; I can eat the whole bag!" They were either unaware of the elevated sugar content in fat-free food, or of how that excess sugar would affect their weight.

Even by reducing our fat intake, we still got fatter because we increased our consumption of simple sugars. This is why it is important not only to *consume less fat*, but also to *reduce simple sugars*, because consumption of simple sugars contributes to weight gain.

BRAIN CHEMISTRY RESPONSE

Once we understand how digestion works, how it affects our brain chemistry, and how metabolism occurs, we can make much better sense of the confusing and often conflicting information we receive regarding proper nutrition. An automobile is equipped with a gas pedal to make it run and a brake pedal to slow it down. The food we eat provides nutrients that perform similar functions in the brain. These nutrients–protein and carbohydrates–link up with specific chemicals in the blood, which enable them to travel to the brain and do their respective jobs. The chart below will help us visualize how this works.

Brain Chemistry Response

Protein *(Gas Pedal)*	**Complex Carbohydrates** *(Brake Pedal)*
Tyrosine *(Amino Acid)*	**Tryptophan** *(Amino Acid)*
Dopamine/Norepinephrine	**Serotonin**

Protein is a "gas pedal" chemical; it speeds up brain transmission. In other words, protein alerts the brain. Our alertness comes from protein. High protein foods include meat, fish, nuts, cheese, and eggs. During digestion, the stomach squeezes the food, extracting the juice. Most of the solid base passes into the intestines and is eventually eliminated as waste. In the meantime, blood comes down to the stomach through the stomach lining and picks up the extracted protein. The blood carries an amino acid called *tyrosine*, which converts the protein into the chemicals *dopamine* and *norepinephrine*, which stimulate and give alertness to the brain.

Because they are alertness chemicals, too much *dopamine* or *norepinephrine* can cause distractibility, hyperactivity, anxiety, and even paranoia. People with Attention Deficit Disorder (ADD) or Attention Deficit Hyperactivity Disorder (ADHD) generally overproduce these chemicals. Being too alert drains our system. Those persons who normally secrete high levels of *dopamine* and *norepinephrine* need to take steps to bring them under control. They need either to reduce the amount of protein they consume or, if that is not practical, possible, or desirable, to exercise consistently to burn off the excess protein. These are the only ways to really limit the protein/tyrosine effect in the body.

On the other side are the complex carbohydrates, which serve as a "brake pedal" for the brain. Basically, complex carbohydrates are fruits, vegetables, and bread, rice, and pasta with color. By "color" I mean whole-grain or multi-grain breads such as wheat, rye, and pumpernickel; "dark" rice such as wild or long-grain; and organic pastas, such as spinach-based. Generally speaking, any "white" carbohydrate, such as white rice or pasta, is less nutritious because of its higher glycemic index–the rate at which it converts to sugar in the blood.

Just as protein speeds up the brain, complex carbohydrates put the brakes on, slowing down brain activity. In other words, they calm the brain. In the blood, complex carbohydrates link up with the amino acid *tryptophan*, which transports them to the brain and converts them to *serotonin*, a chemical that causes us to feel calm, adjusted, and peaceful. People suffering from depression do not produce enough *serotonin*, and often are treated with antidepressant drugs (*serotonin* reuptake inhibitors), which are designed to increase *serotonin* levels in the brain. Basically, complex carbohydrates are natural antidepressants.

Complex carbohydrates are the "good" carbohydrates, the kind that we need continually to fuel our system. Simple carbohydrates, which are everything else–simple sugars, chips, ice cream, candy, pastry, cookies, pie, cake, white bread, fried foods–are the "bad" carbohydrates, and should be consumed in *moderation*. A major part of our problem with obesity and other nutrition-related conditions in America is that our diet is too heavy in simple carbohydrates.

Our body needs complex carbohydrates. When we try to satisfy that need with simple carbohydrates, although we may take care of the immediate craving, what we have actually done is "trick" our body into a sense of satisfaction without really giving it what it needs. Simple carbohydrates simulate the satisfying feeling of complex carbohydrates, but overall have a less healthy effect on the body.

Craving chocolate is a perfect example. Frequently, when discussing nutrition during training, especially with women's groups, I will start out by saying, "It's impossible for you to crave chocolate." Immediately, many of them look at me like they want to burn holes in my stomach. Some people, due in part to variations in body chemistry, do experience feelings that they identify as a chocolate craving, or even addiction, but this is a deception. What I teach in training is that none of us crave chocolate. Our bodies crave complex carbohydrates, but many of us associate that craving with chocolate because, as a simple carbohydrate, it metabolizes rapidly and gives us a quick high. Chocolate, therefore, can become a comfort food.

We need to recognize that when we feel a "craving" for chocolate, our body is really calling out for some type of complex carbohydrate to improve an emotional state. Dark chocolate is better for us and even contains flavonoids that strengthen the immune system like the properties found in wine. Avoiding cocoa butter found in chocolate will also help. Remember, chocolate can produce some good feelings and stimuli, but moderation is the key! Satisfy that need with a piece of fruit, for example, and then, if we desire, we can enjoy a little bit of chocolate.

Our body needs protein and complex carbohydrates. Because it gives us alertness, we should focus on getting most of our protein early in the morning, or at least, in the early part of the day. For the same reason, we should steer away from protein later in the day, especially shortly before bedtime. Even if we are tired enough to go straight to sleep, that late protein will keep the brain active and alert, preventing us from getting the full degree of rest we need, and sometimes even causing us to have weird dreams. Later meals and snacks should focus more on the complex carbohydrate side, because of its calming effect, allowing 60-90 minutes for digestion.

THE EYEBALL METHOD

For the past couple of decades, Americans have been on a "diet craze." There seems to be a national obsession with losing weight. New diets and weight loss plans are popping up all the time. Some of them are good, but many are bogus. Not only do they not work, but some can even be dangerous to our health over the long run. No matter how well conceived or properly balanced a plan may be, in today's fast-paced corporate and social world, most diets do not work for the simple reason that they are too hard to follow. Busy people are not going to count calories. They are not going to measure food portions at every meal. Busy people are not going to keep track of their daily balance between food blocks–a block of protein here, a block of carbohydrates there. I've been in the corporate world long enough to know that it simply is not going to happen in most cases.

At the same time, it is important that we know how to maintain a healthy diet with a proper balance between protein and complex carbohydrates. We need protein for alertness. Complex carbohydrates, which produce *serotonin* for calmness, are important for another reason as well: *energy*. Our physical energy levels come from carbohydrates. During marathon races it is customary for snack stands to be set up along the route so that runners can get a drink of water and something to munch on as they run. One thing those stands never do is offer barbecued ribs or fried chicken, or some other protein source. No, they always provide fruits or vegetables, because the carbohydrates in them provide the energy the runners need.

Some popular diet plans focus on reducing carbohydrate intake while increasing protein. Carbohydrate reduction *is* an effective means of losing weight, but it can also lead to rapid loss of energy. At the same time, increased protein and fat consumption, without sufficient exercise to burn off the excess, can lead to other health and digestion-related problems.

When it comes to a healthy diet, frequency and size of meals are more important than caloric intake. Maintaining a proper balance between protein and carbohydrates has more value than measuring precise portions or weighing fat content. One approach to a balanced diet that I use, and prescribe to performance clients, which is safe and easy to follow, is what I call the *eyeball method*.

Basically, the eyeball method involves learning to look at food with an eye to what it will do in our body, and thus in our brain, over the next three hours. The eyeball method is *intentional fueling*, or fueling our body with the conscious intention of doing the very best we can with each three-hour cycle. Remember the earlier analogy of our body as a high performance vehicle with a small fuel tank. We have to refuel every three hours or eventually we will end up stranded by the roadside. If we are driving on a long road trip, we need to plan our journey in such a way as to have enough fuel to get from one stopping point to the next, as well as allow for periodic rest and recovery breaks. Ignoring either of these will eventually cause trouble down the line.

Our body is equipped with one small fuel tank that needs refilling at frequent and regular intervals, yet many of us eat as if we had multiple reserve and backup tanks. Healthy nutrition is *intentional* nutrition–fueling our body with an eye on its needs for each three-hour cycle rather than on eating primarily for taste or to build up a reserve to get us through long periods of the day. One aspect of peak performance is being lean and agile, carrying only enough fuel to get us successfully from one checkpoint to the next.

Using the eyeball method requires three things. First, we must learn to identify different foods by whether they are primarily a source of protein or a source of carbohydrates. We broke those categories down earlier when we looked at brain chemistry response. Second, we must understand what each food item will do to our system during the three-hour cycle after we eat it. Will it "step on the gas," or "put on the brake"? Third, we must know how any particular food will affect our performance during that same period. Knowledge of these things will enable us to make *informed* and *intentional* decisions regarding what we eat and when.

Here's how it works. It's really pretty simple. Let's say that I am at a restaurant with a buffet. Using the eyeball method, I first want to scope out where the protein foods are (meat, fish, cheese, eggs, lentils, etc.) and where the carbohydrate foods are (fruits, vegetables, breads, pasta,) and so forth. Second, I want to identify the simple from the complex carbohydrates. Next, I want to make my food selection in a manner that will give me a proper protein/carbohydrate ratio.

Generally speaking, the best ratio is one part protein to two parts complex carbohydrates. I need some protein, so perhaps I will choose a chicken breast. Now I need to balance the chicken with some carbohydrates, so I will choose a couple of vegetables, a salad, maybe, and some corn or broccoli. Perhaps I would like some bread also. If it is white bread, as is so often the case in restaurants, I need to keep in mind that it is a simple carbohydrate with less nutritional value. In that case, I may choose to forgo the bread, particularly if I plan to eat dessert, which is also likely to be a simple carbohydrate. If I have two vegetables, some dark bread, perhaps, and a dessert, my meal may be a little heavy on the carbohydrate side and portion size, so to compensate, I might choose some cottage cheese to add to the protein intake I will get from the chicken breast.

In the end, the eyeball method is simply a matter of knowing how much food we need and in what proportions, choosing accordingly, and keeping the portions small, knowing that we will be eating again in three hours. This is really a very simple method that is much easier and more successful than plans that call for measuring and/or weighing food portions. Another advantage of the eyeball method is that it places no foods off limits. By exercising moderation, we can still enjoy all the same foods as before. Within reason, it is okay to take care of those occasional cravings. Just remember to eat sensibly in small portions.

EXERCISE

Regular, consistent exercise stands side by side with sensible nutrition in importance for the health of our body, our physical "vehicle" for navigating life's storms. The health benefits of exercise have long been recognized, as has the connection between exercise and diet for controlling weight and for improving and maintaining overall physical health.

Getting sufficient exercise does not have to be an ordeal, nor does it require an inordinate amount of time, an important consideration for busy people. Here are four simple things that just about anyone in reasonable health can do to ensure they have enough physical activity in their life.

1. *Cardio Training three to four times a week.*

Cardiopulmonary exercise stretches and conditions the heart and the lungs, both of which are critically important. Regular conditioning of our cardiopulmonary system increases our capacity to handle stress. Since stress is *not* going to go away, our best choice is to train ourselves to deal with it. Our bodies are designed for stress, but unless we are properly conditioned, it can still kill us.

Ideally, we should engage in cardiopulmonary conditioning three to four times a week for anywhere from 25 to 40 minutes a session. Three times a week should be the minimum; four times a week is even better. Cardiopulmonary exercise includes such activities as brisk walking, jogging, and bicycling–any activity that will elevate the heart and respiratory rates.

Oscillatory training, which raises and lowers the heart rate in a continuing cycle of stress-recovery, stress-recovery, stress-recovery, is more effective than linear training, which elevates the heart rate and sustains it. Linear training, for example, would be going out and running three miles at a sustained pace. Oscillatory training, on the other hand, might begin with a brisk walk, gradually increase to a fast walk, then to a jog, then a sprint, back to walking, then starting the cycle over again. Most athletes today use this method of training, which is also called *interval training*. Linear training works, but it is not as effective. Interval training generally is more fun to do and easier to sustain than linear training, and it gets us into shape more quickly.

On days that we don't exercise, we need to make sure that we get extra movement. Most of us in the corporate world and elsewhere today don't move around much. We spend our workdays sitting in front of a computer screen or behind a desk. We take the elevator instead of the stairs. We try to park as close to the entrance as possible so we won't have very far to walk.

A simple change in these routines could make a significant difference in our physical condition. Park farther from the door; use the stairs instead of the elevator; stand up every couple of hours and stretch or take a short walk–anything to get extra movement into our daily routine. Any movement we can add to our lifestyle helps our body burn calories, keeps our metabolism running fast, and makes it easier for us to control our weight.

My father worked in a factory for 30 years in a job that required him to be on his feet as much as 12 hours a day. He never "worked out" a day in his life, and yet today, in his 80s, he is in very good shape, especially for someone his age. What is his secret? Simply this: He worked all his life in a job that required constant physical activity. He may not have been exercising, but he was always *moving*.

2. *Stretching*.

In addition to cardiopulmonary exercise, we need to make sure that we stretch on a regular basis. Remember the life toughness markers of *strength*, *flexibility*, and *resilience*. One of the best ways to keep ourselves flexible physically is through regular stretching. This is particularly beneficial on the days we do not exercise, because stretching is a light form of cardiopulmonary activity. If we stretch vigorously, we will work up a sweat. I am talking about simple yoga-type stretching, the kind we can do even while sitting down: stretching our legs out, stretching our arms, twisting our backs, and getting good midsection rotation. Stretching invigorates our muscles and helps us avoid becoming stiff and achy.

3. *Strengthen abdominals.*

The third exercise for optimal physical fitness is a daily regimen of abdominal crunches. Our abdominal muscles serve as "shock absorbers" when we walk or run, and the stronger they are, the better they work. Many people who begin cardiopulmonary training quit after two or three weeks because they develop low back pain. It is not the training itself that causes the pain, but the fact that their abdominal muscles are too weak and out of condition to absorb the shock from the repetitive impact of their feet on the ground as they walk or run. The extra weight slamming repeatedly onto their hips crams their lower back, and they have to stop working out until it heals.

Whenever we take up cardiopulmonary exercise, it is important to work on strengthening our abdominal muscles at the same time. Abdominal crunches are the most effective way to do this, because our abdominal muscles are one of the few muscle groups that we can work every day without harm. Abdominals recover in 12 hours, compared to the 24-36 hours required by other muscle groups.

An abdominal crunch is an oscillatory movement to tighten and strengthen the stomach by "crunching" together the associated muscles in the abdomen. The most basic way to do a crunch is to lie on your back with your legs bent and your feet flat on the floor. This takes the pressure off your lower back. With your hands behind your head and your nose pointed toward the ceiling, bend slightly at the waist in a series of controlled curls, scrunching the abdominal muscles together. These are *small* movements, not sit-ups. Keep your neck straight; don't let your hands pull your head and neck up. Let your abdominals do the work. These curls are so slight that your shoulder blades should not even leave the floor. A series of 20-30 of these a day working up to 100 a day is optimal.

4. *Resistance training.*

To round out our exercise regimen, we need *resistance training* three to four times a week–weightlifting, nautilus machine, body resistance, pushups, curls, etc. An elastic "dynaband" or exercise band is useful to keep on hand because it is so versatile. It can be used to work biceps, triceps, chest, back, and even legs. I keep one in my bag and use it often while on the road.

Choose whatever approach works best for you, whether to work out at the gym or at home, to use special equipment or to use none. The important thing is to be consistent, working your resistance training three to four times a week, for about 30-40 minutes a session. That should be sufficient for most people.

REST/RECHARGE AND HYDRATION

Our training to take proper care of our body is not complete until we give adequate attention to our need for regular rest and recovery and hydration. In music, the rests are just as important as the notes. The same is true in life. None of us can exercise all the time, nor should we. Unlike the Energizer® bunny, we can't keep going and going and going without a break. We have to have time to recover and recharge. In addition to balanced nutrition, we need to make sure we drink plenty of water throughout the day.

1. *R & R every 90 minutes.*

Throughout this book I have stressed the need for us to get rest and recovery every 90 minutes. I mention it again here because we cannot afford to underestimate its importance. Our physiology operates on 90-minute oscillatory cycles, and we should strive to include in each cycle some splash of rest and recharge or recovery. Ninety minutes is ideal; two hours is the maximum window. After two hours our acuities in every area begin to fall off rapidly.

Two to five minutes is all that is necessary for these recovery breaks. Take a walk, chat with someone, sing, pray, grab a quick nap, meditate, get a drink of water, eat if a meal or snack time coincides with a break, listen to some music. Anything like this that breaks a stress cycle for a few minutes is good for recovery. The important thing is to do it consistently.

2. *Hydrate all during the day.*

Most Americans do not drink enough water. Dehydration affects our ability to perform in every area. It is important not only to drink sufficient amounts of water, but also to spread it out through the day. Depending on our height, weight, build, and gender, we should drink anywhere from 32-48 ounces of water daily. It's alright to drink other things as well, but we need to make sure we have a sufficient water table. In this as in every other area, moderation is the key.

3. *Monitor daily sleep times and patterns.*

Another important part of regular rest and recovery is to monitor and regulate our daily sleep times and patterns as much as possible. Sleep deprivation is an ongoing problem for many Americans. Because of Brandon's condition, my wife and I live with sleep deprivation issues on a daily basis. It is one of the *life storms* that we have had to learn to navigate.

Rhythm and oscillatory cycles—the so-called "body clock"—are built into our physiology, and it is important that we learn to work *with* them, not *against* them. Too often our sleep cycle and habits run counter to our body's natural rhythm, leaving us feeling tired all the time, even after what we thought was a good night's sleep, and negatively affecting our alertness and ability to perform well. Although we can adapt our body clock to different conditions, such as shift work or jobs that require unusually long periods of wakefulness and activity, generally we are better off sleeping while the sun is down, because that is the way our system is designed to work.

The more routine we can build into our sleep pattern, the better. Here are some useful tips.

- Go to bed at the same time each night and get up at the same time every morning. Your body will quickly adjust to this routine, making it easier both to fall asleep quickly and to wake up refreshed and ready to go.
- Shut down mental and emotional stimuli half an hour before bedtime. Turn off the TV, don't watch the news immediately before going to bed, avoid any activity that will shift your brain into analytical mode.
- If reading before bed, make sure it is leisure reading, not required or work-related reading: a novel or other book of personal interest, a hobby magazine, poetry, a collection of short stories, religious literature, etc.—anything that will help relax and unwind your mind.

- Do not eat anything later than 90 minutes before bedtime. This allows time for your digestive system to settle down.
- Make sure that your bedroom and bed are as comfortable as possible. The room temperature should be cooler rather than warmer, because it is easy to compensate for a cool room with extra covers and blankets.
- Try to sleep with all the lights off. If you need some light, use a nightlight. Regular light will stimulate your senses too much, waking you up and making it hard to get back to sleep.
- Avoid looking at the clock during the night. Reading the time will be filed as data in the left brain, stimulating it to analytical hyper mode. Peaceful sleep will be hindered because the left brain will be saying, "What should I do with this information–file it, process and fix it, or forget it?"
- When it is time to get up, get up without delay, turn on the lights, and get active immediately. Some light in the morning is good, especially sunlight. It helps you wake up.

For travelers, here are some helpful hints regarding jet lag:

- Make sure you hydrate properly. Aircraft cabins have very dry air, which can dehydrate the body. Drink plenty of water and/or juice. Avoid alcohol or caffeine because these are diuretics, which will only add to the dehydration problem.
- When flying across time zones, particularly west to east, set your watch for the time zone of your destination. This will help your body clock start adjusting in that direction.

- Try to nap during part of the flight, or at least relax with your eyes closed.
- When you arrive at your destination, obey the time in that place. In other words, go to bed at the same time locally as you normally would at home. When you wake up the following morning, you will be pretty much on track.

4. *Prepare to arrive home.*

The best kind of rest and recovery is the kind we deliberately plan for. This is especially true when making the transition from work mode to home mode. A helpful approach is to use at least part of the commute home to shift gears mentally and emotionally. If we spend the entire trip home doing what we have done all day in the office–talking on the cell phone to clients, customers, or workers; making deals and decisions; and taking care of last-minute or "urgent" details–we will likely continue in the same mode when we get home. Walking into the house in full executive or management mode, and barking out orders to everyone in sight is no way to treat our family. If we take time to shift into "home" gear, we will feel better when we get there, and so will our family members.

Peak Performance vs. Compromised Performance

Below is a chart that graphically illustrates the difference between peak performance and compromised performance.

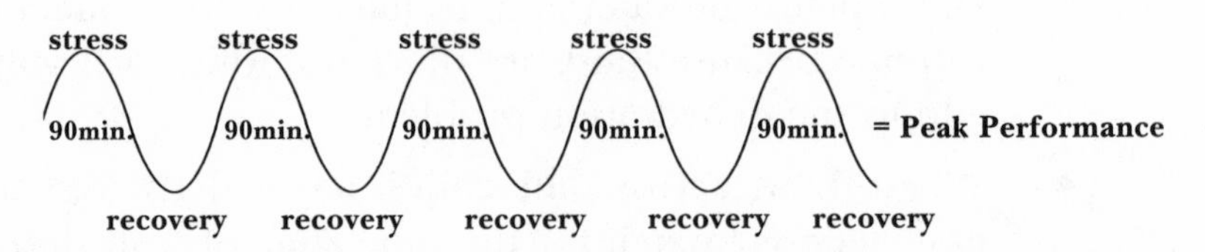

= Compromised Performance

One way to look at these two graphs is to imagine them as readouts of an electrocardiogram (EKG) or electroencephalogram (EEG). Graph number one represents a *good day*, but graph number two represents a *really BAD day*!

Peak performance requires that we oscillate in 90-minute cycles of stress-recovery, stress-recovery, stress-recovery. Each peak and valley pair in the first graph represents that 90-minute window. That's the way our body normally operates, and our key to peak performance is to work with that cycle, not against it. The first graph represents a measured, structured approach to the day. That's the way I have learned to operate. I lay out my day in 90-minute segments, and even think in those terms. It is so much easier to deal with the day in cycles. Work a cycle, take a break to refocus and recover, work a cycle, take a break, etc. throughout the day.

Graph number two, the flat line moving to the right, represents compromised performance, based on a linear approach to the day. It illustrates the attitude of jumping into the day and going full throttle without a stop all day long. We have eight or ten hours of work ahead of us, so we just plunge right in and plow through. This is the attitude so prevalent in corporate America today which, if it does not kill us, at least greatly hinders both our daily and long-term performance. It simply isn't worth it.

Peak performance in the physical zone depends upon a proper balance between nutrition, conditioning, and rest and recovery. We often underestimate the importance of one or another of these elements, especially the last one, and fail to recognize the significance of the link between them. Of all the people I have known and worked with in sports science over the years, Emerson Fittapaldi stands out as one of the best examples of this physical balance.

A champion Brazilian race car driver who is now retired, Emerson Fittapaldi drove in the Formula One racing circuit for years, and is a past winner in F1 and the Indianapolis 500. We got to know him in Detroit, where he came every year for the Detroit Grand Prix. He was drawn to Brandon from the start. We would talk to Emerson and have lunch with him. He even gave us the chance to go down into the pit and check out his race car. Once, he put Brandon in the car and we took pictures. He autographed hats, shirts, and photographs and gave them to us. Brandon really touched Emerson's life. He has an unbelievable amount of stuff from Emerson.

What really impressed me about Emerson was the way he prepared himself for a race. Before a big race, and even before qualifying heats, his routine was the same. He would put on his racing suit, leave it unzipped at the top for comfort, and then find some place to stretch out. Emerson would actually *go to sleep*. Upon waking, he would zip his suit up, put his helmet on, not talk to anyone, get in his car, and drive his fastest laps.

He had developed such a ritual that he would relax his body, go to sleep, and wake up completely focused on his race plan. He would not talk or give interviews if possible. He would not go over his notes time and time again; he had done that at pre-race meetings. He would simply get in his car and drive like no one else could. Emerson Fittapaldi is a testimony to the power of recovery before a performance.

Chapter Seven

Copilot Navigation

No man is an island, entire of itself;
every man is a piece of the continent, a part of the main.

–John Donne

So far we have examined life navigation from the angle of improving our personal performance by training and sharpening our *mental*, *emotional*, *spiritual*, and *physical* acuities. We have studied principles and commonsense steps to help us learn how to process stress and use it to propel us to consistent excellence–to perform *under pressure, on demand.*

Now we need to consider how our performance affects our *copilots*, those people who are making the journey with us. Rarely is the navigation of life's storms a solo trip. The 17th-century English poet John Donne was right when he wrote, "*No man is an island, entire of itself; every man is a piece of the continent, a part of the main.*" Our performance, attitude, words, actions, and behavior influence all the people we have relationships with, whether family, friends, or work colleagues.

The key to successful *copilot navigation*–flying with other people–is learning to think and function as a member of a team. A family is a team. A company is a team. Any group of people who have joined together for the purpose of achieving a common goal is, (or should be), a team. *Copilot navigation* involves assessing and improving our effectiveness on the team. We can also call this the *discovery zone*.

US Navy SEALS have a unique concept of team leadership. A SEAL team could consist of a few to several teammates with different ranks and expertise. For example, one individual on the team may be a jump specialist, though he may be the lowest ranking SEAL on the team. However, because of his particular expertise, he becomes the lead man for this element of the operational mission, with everyone else on the team including the lead command officer yielding to his leadership. The next element of the opp might be a night dive, and the dive specialist would lead this phase; the next element might require the marksman specialist to lead, until that phase is complete. At the end of each element opp, the lead officer resumes command until all the necessary elements are complete, using the best man for that specific phase of the mission. How much better would our families, communities, governments, and companies be if we could lay down egos and self-interest for the sake of completing the mission handed to us. We should all learn a valuable lesson from the elite performers of the SEALs and claim victory, with limited casualties and maximized performance.

In the weeks and months following September 11, 2001, I witnessed countless examples of Americans pulling together as teams. At Ground Zero, the selfless efforts of hundreds of firefighters, police officers, rescue personnel, FEMA workers, construction workers, and ordinary New Yorkers working together to recover from this tragedy was truly inspiring. I saw the same spirit in Americans all across the country as I traveled from place to place leading workshops and doing training.

Nothing brings out the team spirit in Americans better than a crisis. What affects one of us affects us all. In 1941, Americans were divided as to whether or not the nation should get involved in the global war that had already been raging for two years. Then came December 7, when the Japanese launched a surprise attack on Pearl Harbor. Overnight, the division virtually disappeared as Americans put aside their differences and joined together as a team to defeat a common enemy.

THE GRIEVING PROCESS

Our effectiveness in *copilot navigation* depends to a large degree on our ability to process and navigate our personal storms. One characteristic element that is common to most life storms is grief. To one extent or another we grieve whenever we experience a loss of any kind. The intensity of our grief varies according to the worth or value of what was lost as well as our emotional distance from it. The loss of a loved one, a job, a pet, a cherished dream–we grieve at different levels for all of these, but in each case the grief is real.

On September 11, 2001, America went into national grieving. As we have worked through our grief as a nation, we have passed through all the same typical stages of the grieving process that individuals undergo. The first stage is *shock*. As soon as this tragedy occurred, we as a nation went into shock mode. This is a completely natural and normal response that temporarily deadens our senses and helps prevent us from hurting or destroying ourselves in some way.

After a few days, the numbness wore off and we entered the second stage, *catharsis*, where we began to vent our emotions. *Catharsis* is the part of grieving where we find ourselves crying, feeling intense emotional pain, and often a certain detachment from society, friends, and family.

It is common after catharsis to enter a period of *depression* where we may even feel a sense of guilt or personal responsibility for what happened. This is the "if only" stage: "If only I had been there, I could have done something more"; "If only I hadn't said that, then none of this would have happened," etc. In truth, there may be (and probably is) very little we could actually have done to change the situation or prevent the tragedy, but we feel that way nonetheless.

Extended preoccupation with loss can be dangerous to *mental*, *emotional*, *spiritual*, and *physical* health. Over time, the intensity of the sense of loss begins to dissipate, but quite often it first manifests through the stage of *anger*. Once the shock of the September 11 attacks had worn off and we had a chance to vent our grief and sorrow as a nation, those feelings changed to anger toward those who had perpetrated the criminal acts. Prolonged uncontrolled anger is very dangerous. Remember the high negative emotional quadrant with its high-level release of *cortisol*, which has such a devastating effect on the immune system. High negative emotions adversely affect not only the people around us, but also our own ability to navigate life, as well as our ability to form and maintain effective relationships with others.

The final stage of grief, and the one that shows that healing is taking place, is *acceptance of reality*. This is when we fully and readily acknowledge all that has happened, and how we feel about it, and decide that the time has come to move on with life. How long we spend in each stage of grief will depend on the magnitude of the loss, our individual personality and temperament, and how well-trained and equipped we are to process our grief. The time we take to move through each stage is not as important as monitoring our progress to make sure that we *keep moving*. Grief is a natural response to loss, but it is *not* natural to get *stuck* in the process. Unresolved grief will short-circuit our ability to navigate, which will also adversely affect our *copilots.*

RELATIONAL LUBRICATION

Relationships are a key part of life. Unless we exile ourselves on a desert island somewhere, we cannot get through life without dealing with relationships in some form or another. No matter where we are–at home, at work, at school, at the grocery store, at the mall–if we are around people, we have to navigate relationships. Whether that trip is smooth or bumpy depends on how well we understand the dynamics of a relationship and our particular role in it.

In almost any relational arrangement, we must consider three elements, what we could call the "*I, we, it*" system. *I* refers to the *individual* component: you, me, another person; any individual who is involved in a relationship. *We* is the *team* element: two or more people working together. *It* refers to the *organization* that the individuals and teams are a part of. At the domestic level, for example, a husband, a wife, and their children are *individuals*, collectively they are a *team*, and the family is their *organization*. In the corporate world, each employee is an *individual* who is part of a specific office, division, or work group (the *team*) in a larger company, which is the *organization*. In any situation, the way to best serve the *it* is by taking care of the *I* and working well with the *we*.

Any smoothly operating machine needs good lubrication. If you try to drive your car without oil in the engine, you won't drive it very long. The engine block will overheat, the pistons will seize up, and your engine will become nothing more than several hundred pounds of useless metal. Relationships are no different; they require regular lubrication as well. When it comes to smooth relationships, nothing is more important than effective communication. Communication is *relational lubrication*, the "oil" that keeps our relationships from burning up.

At a very basic level, communication is about *connecting* with others. It is a lot like playing catch. If I throw a ball to you and you catch it, we have connected. If you throw it back and I catch it, the connection is even more complete. However, if I throw the ball and you are not looking, and it bounces off your head, we have not made a connection. Movement has occurred only in one direction.

Communication *always* involves *dialogue*, a two-way flow of information between a sender and a receiver. As a sender, I speak to you, and as a receiver, you respond back to me. That way I will know whether or not you have understood me. Without understanding, there is no communication. Once you respond to me, you become a sender, and I become a receiver, who then responds to *your* response. *Monologue*, or a one-way flow of information is not really communication, because there is no response or feedback to determine whether or not understanding has taken place.

Some Truths About Training

If any training is to be effective, there must be good communication between the trainer and the trainees. Whether we are in a position to *receive* training or to *train* others, there are several important truths we should remember that will help keep the channels of communication open as well as help to ensure that the training is successful.

1. *Management and leadership are very different things. Things* require *management*, but *people* require *leadership*. We *manage* spreadsheets, financial data, inventory, contracts, and computer systems, but we *lead* people. Managing people

suggests the idea of employees working while someone constantly looks over their shoulders saying, "You missed that," or "You forgot to cross that 'T' and dot that 'I.' " No one likes to work under that kind of "management," and few people perform well—never mind about performing their best—under those circumstances.

Leadership, on the other hand, paints the picture and then says to the people, "Go do it." Good leadership provides guidelines and principles, but allows much room for individual talent, initiative, and creativity. Effective leaders are not only visionaries, but also possess the ability to *inspire* others with the vision and thereby make it their own.

2. *Remember that the best athletes in the world have* ***coaches***. Some people might say, "I don't need any help, I don't need any accountability in my life, and I don't need a coach. I know what I need to do." Self-reliance is one thing; this attitude, however, is a recipe for failure. Tiger Woods has coaches. Michael Jordan has coaches. Not only do the best athletes in the world have coaches, they recognize better than anyone else that they *need* coaches. That is one of the reasons why they are the best in the world; they never stop learning, they never stop trying to improve. None of us should ever stop learning. Peak performers are always striving to learn more and to get better at what they do. They constantly compete against themselves, seeking always to run a little faster, jump a little higher, and advance a little farther than last time.

3. *If you are* ***in*** *the game you cannot* ***see*** *the game!* This is another reason why coaches are important. When we are right in the thick of things, it is hard, if not impossible, to constantly maintain a balanced view either of the situation or of our own capabilities. We need someone to help us who has a

visual-spatial perspective on what is happening. That is what a coach provides.

4. *We will not consistently outperform our **training**.* In other words, we must *train* in the same way we expect to *play* or *perform*. We can't continually blow off study and preparation and expect to do well. As a general rule, our performance will be only as effective as our training. We should set our sights high and train with the goal in view.

Broadway performers are notorious for their hard work, but it pays off with many stunning performances on stage. Top athletes, whether amateur or professional, put in long, demanding hours in training that spectators rarely see, just so they can shine for a few minutes with an over-the-top performance in their chosen sport. The well-known adage is true: "No pain, no gain." We will not consistently outperform our training.

5. *A 30-day commitment with tough **coaching** is necessary to accomplish goals and keep them a reality.* Any permanent change in our life requires 30 days to take hold. If, for instance, we want to institute a balanced nutrition and exercise program, we will need to follow it consistently for 30 days in order for it to become part of us.

Changing habits or lifestyle is a *push-pull* cycle. Until we have practiced the change or new discipline consistently for 30 days, it will be a *push* for us. We will have to fight to maintain the change, because old habits die hard. If we are used to staying in bed a few extra minutes in the morning, we will have to *push* ourselves to get up early enough for the cardiopulmonary or resistance training that we have committed to. If we have a frequent strong hankering for pizza, we will have to *push* ourselves to opt for a salad instead.

After we have practiced the change consistently for 30 to 45 days, a transition will occur where the *push* becomes a *pull*, and we find ourselves drawn to the new behavior instead of the old. Now we feel *pulled* to work out and *pulled* for that salad, because we have experienced the benefits for ourselves. Building systematic change into our lives by sticking with it long enough to get from *push* to *pull* is easier when we can align the desired changes with our *life purpose*. If we know *why* the change is important, the inspiration and motivation to make it happen are easier to find.

WHAT LIMITS *YOUR* PERFORMANCE?

Let's do an exercise. Study the list below and identify as many performance-limiting characteristics as you feel apply to you. If there is a characteristic of your life that you really struggle with that is not listed here, include it. Take your time and be honest with yourself. Before you can make meaningful change in your life, you have to identify the problem areas.

Limiting Performance List

Circle any that apply:

- Poor team player
- Low energy levels
- Poor follow-through
- Low motivation
- Poor leadership
- Negative thinking
- Poor fitness
- Chronic fatigue
- Poor work-life balance
- Mental/Body inflexibility

- Insensitive to others
- Short temper
- Poor sleep habits (a.m. fatigue)
- Fear or paranoia
- Lack of trust in others

List three obstacle behaviors that are compromising daily peak performance. Choose ONE obstacle to begin your journey:

- ______________________________
- ______________________________
- ______________________________

What are the things that you are really dealing with in your life? What habits, characteristics, or behaviors limit your performance? Identify as many as necessary. From your initial list, choose the three that create the most problems for you as far as consistent high performance is concerned. Narrow that list down to the one area you want to deal with *first*. The whole point of this exercise is to develop an awareness of where your biggest challenges lie, and to put into place a specific plan for addressing those challenges.

Generally, we are more successful in affecting change in our lives when we keep a sharp and narrow focus. If we try to juggle too many things at once, we will probably drop all of them, and give up in discouragement. That's the reasoning behind choosing one item at a time.

There is an old proverb that says that the way to eat an elephant is one bite at a time. Beginning with the first item on your list, concentrate on it exclusively over the next 30 to 45 days until you get it down. Then, move to item number two and do the same thing. Follow up with item three. It will take anywhere from three to five months to complete the change in three areas. This is not necessarily a fast process, but the changes will be more successful and permanent. Thirty to forty-five days allows sufficient time for the new habits or behaviors to get loaded into the autonomic nervous system where, under a subconscious triggering mechanism, they become second nature.

ACTION PLAN

Identifying and targeting a specific goal for change and improvement is important, but to ensure success you need an action plan, a system to follow every day during the 30 to 45-day period in which you are focused on implementing a specific change. Such a plan is given below. Notice that some of the elements of the plan are items we have discussed earlier. This is deliberate because all of these things are interconnected.

THIRTY-DAY LIFE NAVIGATION SYSTEM

1. *START each day with Purpose Alignment.* As we have already seen, this is pretty simple. At the beginning of your day each morning, take two to five minutes–longer if needed–to align yourself by identifying what is most important for you that day. Zero in on that bull's-eye in your life from which flow your *passion*, *motivation*, *perseverance*, and *force*.

2. *R&R every 90 minutes.* There is no need to say anything more here except a reminder that this element is too important to ignore. Don't bypass this step; you will only shortchange yourself and frustrate your goals in the long run.

3. *JOURNAL daily progress.* Take time each evening to assess your progress during the day by rating yourself (*low*, *average*, or *high*) in the areas of purpose, nutrition, exercise, energy, and recovery. How did you do in each area throughout the day? Are you on track, or is there some area that

needs more attention? Were you passionate in your purpose today? Did you make wise choices for your meals and snacks? Did you get your exercise today? How were your energy levels? Did you remember to take your recovery breaks?

Below is a chart that I use in training to help with daily journalizing. Use it to track your progress and keep an ongoing record for day-by-day comparison. This will help you see where you are improving, where you may be stalled, or where you may be falling back.

Coaching Accountability Chart

Rating Scale **1**-Low **2**-Average **3**-High

WEEK	PURPOSE	NUTRITION	EXERCISE	ENERGY	RECOVERY
Sunday					
Monday					
Tuesday					
Wednesday					
Thursday					
Friday					
Saturday					

Another helpful part of this process is to find someone you trust and respect who will agree to be your coach, or at least to hold you accountable from day to day and week to week. We need some accountability to help us stay focused on our goal. Implementing change into our lives is always easier when there is some interested party encouraging and cheering us on from the sidelines.

TRAINING MAKES THE DIFFERENCE

Chaos and *life storms* are normal parts of life, regardless of how they look or feel. We will never completely escape from them. With proper training, however, we can navigate them successfully, and even prosper from them.

Early in my psychology training, I interned as a crisis phone counselor in Detroit, Michigan for two years. During my first week I fielded three suicide calls. One of the callers informed me that he had a gun pointed to his head and was going to pull the trigger unless I could tell him something that would help him.

Thank God for good training! My first response from training was to use some humor to break his focus on self-inflicting bodily harm. I said, "Please don't pull that trigger because I don't want the sound ringing in my ear." It is said that timing is everything. After a moment of silence during which the caller processed my comment, he snickered and asked, "Are you crazy?" "Not today," I replied, "but I can relate to how you feel."

My pointed statement changed his focus long enough to allow me to connect with him and effectively communicate to him that other people cared about him and so did I. We spoke for quite a while and, in the meantime, following emergency protocol, a first response team was deployed to his home to assist him.

After the phone call ended, and I came to my senses, I realized how close I had come to witnessing firsthand a suicide during my watch. My next thought was how well I had been trained to function in chaos, and how not to panic, but to trust my training instincts to help me reach out with compassion and render assistance. Since that early training experience, I have learned to thrive in chaos, knowing that *chaos is only a temporary transition to a more permanent solution.* Chaos, defined as "transitional change," is inevitable, but with proper training and focus, the fear that potentially can block forward progress, can transform into courage to enable us to charge like a warrior into harm's way in order to make a difference.

Some time ago my younger son, Brent, traveled to New York with a group of other young people from West Palm Beach to assist families affected by the 9/11 tragedy. Although he was excited to see New York and all it has to offer, he was not totally prepared for the emotional upheaval that would occur after a week at Ground Zero. The first night he spent at the site and meeting many of the families who lost loved ones there overwhelmed his senses. His first phone call home was mainly just to check in and update us on the events of his day, but with his voice trembling and his thoughts focused on the grief and loss he had witnessed there, he ended up explaining every detail to us.

I remember him saying, "Hey Dad, I love you. You know that, right?" I replied, "Of course I do, son!" Brent went on to share how he could now relate to all my visits to Ground Zero trying to help and train survivors, since he had seen firsthand how many lives were touched on that terrible day. He shared how bad he felt at seeing so many kids of all ages who had lost one or both parents, and how thankful he was just to talk to us on the phone. I am convinced that after sharing in the pain and the healing process of so many who were less fortunate than himself, and because of all that he learned during the experience, Brent will never again be the same.

Brent's experience and mine emphasize once again how exposure to stress, chaos, grief, and pain can be the stimulus for healthy growth if processed correctly with the proper training. The Lyles family training ground is replete with daily pain and suffering because of Brandon's disabilities and the slow motion struggles of life and death that come with terminal illness. However, that pain training ground has toughened our family in ways that we usually do not notice until a crisis comes. That is when we realize anew how important life training is for all of us.

Since reality is 90 percent perception, we all have unlimited access and opportunity to grow in a healthy way, and respond well to the most challenging times and events of our lives. Think for a moment. What life experiences have made you the toughest and strongest? Were they not the periods of your greatest struggles and difficulties? Learning to process stress and make it work for us is a powerful tool in helping us become well-rounded and highly gifted individuals able to deliver consistent high performance in any situation.

LIVING WITH NO REGRETS

As I look back on my life from where I am today, I can honestly say now that I would not change anything. The total mix of my life, all the good, the bad, and the ugly through the years, has served to train me and define me very specifically into the person I am today. When I was growing up, I got into some trouble and made some poor decisions (who hasn't?) before I got my life straightened out, but those experiences help me empathize today with people who are where I once was.

Although I would never wish to repeat the stormy times, I would not trade those experiences for anything in the world, because they helped me learn about life. My life has not been perfect or always smooth, but as I look back, *I have no regrets* about my past because my past has shaped who I am today. In the present, I want to *live today with no regrets*; to live in such a way as to go to my grave with no music left in me. I want to live such a life that in the future *I will have no regrets* about how I spent my time.

Over the years I have talked to many elderly people who have expressed regrets about things they wish they had done but didn't, places they wish they had gone but didn't, time they could have spent with their children but didn't. Some have expressed a wish that they had spent more money on worthy causes and saved less so that their children wouldn't be fighting over the inheritance.

I don't want to be that way at the end of my life. I want to live—and die—without regrets. I want to do what is in my heart to do every day, one day at a time, for a lifetime. Have I made mistakes? Of course I have. Will I continue to make mistakes? Of course I will. That's part of life. I do not fear failing, but I *do* fear *not trying*. Failure is scary, but it is also an essential step on the pathway to success. All of us fail at one time or another, but as long as we fail *forward*, as John Maxwell says, we are at least six feet closer to our goal. Living without regret does not mean we will never fail, but it does mean we will never fail because of *not trying*. That is why I start every day with purpose alignment. It is why I make sure to get periodic recovery every day. I don't want to waste a moment. Time is precious, and life is short.

I believe that if we are not "living on the edge," we are taking up space, and it may be someone else's space. Life on the edge is exciting and daring, and certainly never boring. Fear often drives us to live in the safety net of the mainstream, which dulls our acuities and prevents our full potential, skill, and talent from coming out. Life is risky on the edge, but the edge is where we can become all that we can be. We make more mistakes on the edge, and can fall a long way before grabbing hold of solid ground again, but the edge is where the greatest challenges and opportunities lie.

Living with no regrets means living with *passion*, being *passionate* about everything we do, so that our lives will affect other people *passionately*. Living with no regrets means striving to be the *tip* of the arrow, the first to hit the target, the one to make the deepest impact on others.

To live a life with no regrets is to live a *balanced* life *mentally*, *emotionally*, *spiritually*, and *physically* regardless of the *life storms*. It is to develop *life toughness* through *strength*, *flexibility*, and *resilience*. Living with no regrets means understanding our instrument gauges and what they are saying to us. It means flying with our radar–our spiritual acuity–at highest sensitivity so that we can continually see the larger scope of our *life purpose*. Finally, living with no regrets means taking care of our bodies through proper *nutrition*, *exercise*, *rest and recovery*, *sleep cycles*, and adequate *hydration* of water every day. This will enable us to become the optimal performers that we need to be in order to do our jobs the very best that we can possibly do them, *under pressure*, *on demand*.

Additional Guidelines and Notes

Author Contact

You may contact the author at:

1-800-375-9537

or visit his Web site at:

www.terrylyles.com

For more information/education and products concerning nutritional wellness contact:

Garden of Life, Inc.
770 Northpoint Parkway
Suite 100
West Palm Beach, FL 33407

561-748-2477
www.gardenoflifeusa.com

Additional copies of this book and other book titles from DESTINY IMAGE are available at your local bookstore.

For a bookstore near you, call 1-800-722-6774

Send a request for a catalog to:

Destiny Image® Publishers, Inc.
P.O. Box 310
Shippensburg, PA 17257-0310

"Speaking to the Purposes of God for This Generation and for the Generations to Come"

For a complete list of our titles, visit us at www.destinyimage.com